Us Women, Our Ways, Our World

Us Women, Our Ways, Our World

Edited by Pat Dudgeon, Jeannie Herbert,
Jill Milroy and Darlene Oxenham

Magabala Books

First published 2017
Magabala Books Aboriginal Corporation, Broome, Western Australia
website: www.magabala.com Email: sales@magabala.com

Magabala Books receives financial assistance from the Commonwealth Government through the Australia Council, its arts advisory body. The State of Western Australia has made an investment in this project through the Department of Culture and the Arts in Association with LotteryWest. Magabala Books would like to acknowledge the support of the Shire of Broome, Western Australia.

Cover design by Greg Jorss, Upside Creative

Cover illustration (and details used throughout the book): *Mungit Dreaming* by Elaine Cox. *Mungit Dreaming* is about strong Mungit Women from the Dampier Peninsula who lived off the land. The lizard (mungit) represents the Mungit Family Totem, the fish represents food gathered by the Mungit Women, and the people figures are the Mungit Women.

Printed by Griffin Press, South Australia

Cataloguing-in-publication data available from the
National Library of Australia

ISBN 9781925360509

Government of Western Australia Department of Culture and the Arts | lotterywest supported | Australian Government | Australia Council for the Arts | Shire of Broome people · place · prosperity

NOTE FROM THE EDITORS ON TERMINOLOGY

The terms 'Indigenous', 'Aboriginal', 'Aboriginal and Torres Strait Islander' are used interchangeably throughout this book and are intended to be inclusive of all groups as they relate to specific communities. Their use in this book is reflective of how they have been used by the contributors to this project.

Similarly, the spelling of the name of the traditional owners of the Southwest of Western Australia – Noongar, Nyungar, Nyoongah, vary between authors but refer to the same collective group.

CONTENTS

PREFACE

This book has sought to honour Aboriginal and Torres Strait Islander women's perspectives and standpoints in a unique and innovative way. It is the culmination of considerable discussions and a willingness to take a different approach to presenting the stories of the individual authors. The editors, Pat Dudgeon, Jill Milroy, Darlene Oxenham and Jeannie Herbert, all Aboriginal academics with a long history of working in Aboriginal and Torres Strait Islander programs in Australian universities, believed that a critical strategy in 'closing the disadvantage gap' between Australia's Indigenous peoples and those who have come to this country from other nations, was to find a way in which Aboriginal and Torres Strait Islander women could share their personal perspectives with other Australian women. Having recognised the need to enable the voices of Aboriginal women to be heard, however, they also realised the critical importance of doing this in a way that would allow the diversity of those voices to come through. All agreed that, as individuals, their life and professional experiences had demonstrated the importance of acknowledging the collective equality of Aboriginal women's voices, regardless of where people came from or what they did. It was deemed impossible to understand Aboriginal people and their place in the Australian story without having some knowledge of the different stories, and the depth and breadth of them nurtured over several generations. Hence, the decision was made to put together a literary text with a difference, a book that would bring together the voices of Aboriginal women in a way that would clearly demonstrate to the wider community that regardless of where Aboriginal women came from, where they lived or had lived, their level of previous education within both Aboriginal and Western contexts, their lifestyle or their age, all had the right to speak and to know their voices were equally valued.

This book comprises a collection of stories from Aboriginal women from around the country. Many were raised in small, isolated communities while others grew up in urban locations. While most of the contributors work in Australian universities, many have come into this sector from a wide variety of other working experiences within the public and private sectors. Regardless of their different personal histories, their stories are all situated in the context of their identities as Aboriginal women. From this gendered location as Indigenous people, the perspectives presented in this book have common themes highlighting the importance of family and other relationships; of knowing who they are and how they came to be that person; and of recognising the continuing impact of this country's colonial history and the constant struggle to overcome the insidious racism that is deeply embedded in Australian society. Importantly, flowing through all the stories is an incredible strength to survive and thrive in oppressive spaces both historical and contemporary that underpins but also reflects each writer's deep pride in their Aboriginality. This critical element has enabled individuals not only to survive but, in fact, to become increasingly resilient in the face of ongoing adversity.

This book was considered as a means of demonstrating to educators generally, but most particularly those in the higher education sector, that all students need to be able to hear from a diversity of Indigenous voices if they are to really understand Aboriginal and Torres Strait Islander peoples. Exposure to the diversity of the writers' voices offered in this book will enable readers to understand where these women are coming from – the life experiences that have influenced them determine how they have been positioned within the wider Australian society and what have been the long-term impacts of this nation's colonial history.

PROFESSOR DARLENE OXENHAM is Malgana from the Shark Bay region in Western Australia. She joined the School of Indigenous Studies at the University of Western Australia in February 2006 as Associate Dean, Teaching and Learning and now holds the position of Deputy Dean. Previously, Darlene held concurrent positions at the Centre for Aboriginal Studies at Curtin University as Deputy Head of Centre, Director of the Curtin Indigenous Research Centre and Coordinator of the Honours and Postgraduate Programs. Darlene has been involved in Aboriginal higher education for 20 years.

PROFESSOR JILL MILROY is Palyku from the Pilbara region of Western Australia. Jill is Pro Vice Chancellor Indigenous Education at the Univerisity of Western Australia. She has more than 30 years experience in Indigenous higher education developing programs and support services for Indigenous students as well as a range of Indigenous curriculum and research initiatives. Jill has served on a number of national policy advisory bodies and in 2011 was appointed a Member of the Order of Australia in recognition of her services to Indigenous education. Her key research interest is in Aboriginal knowledge, history, place and story systems.

INTRODUCTION

Darlene Oxenham and Jill Milroy

In producing this publication we, the editors, sought to acknowledge what the contributors perceived to be the particular strengths of Australia's Aboriginal women. In seeking to explore the diversity that exists within the cohort of Aboriginal women and how such diversity might impact on the way we engage with one another, both individually and collectively, the book has revealed some fascinating insights into what Aboriginal women have to offer the world.

The value that Aboriginal women place on relationships emanates throughout the book. Indeed, the book is a product and reflection of the relationships built and sustained over many years between the authors. We are all connected through education and all have some association with universities. For us, an integral component of relationships is understanding that we have to get our voice out there, to support other women to make change in Aboriginal society and to recognise what we are contributing to advancing our communities as a whole.

Several authors highlight the value of relationships – grandmother, mother, daughter, aunt, and sister and sisterhood relationships. Mary Terszac, for example, clearly describes the importance of 'mother' and the profound sense of loss if that relationship is taken away, while Cheryl Kickett-Tucker writes with and about her mother Shirley Harris and the story of their family. What shines through in this chapter is the importance and centrality of family and the mother-daughter bond that is undoubtedly strong and proud. This is quite beautiful to read given the many images and stories that appear in various media programs on Aboriginal people and dysfunctional families. This chapter radiates familial love and a gentle determination to maintain and sustain this by passing it on to future generations of Aboriginal women and their families. Cheryl explains the strength and spirit of Aboriginal women is such that 'we must remain strong, reliable and responsible despite being challenged with life's hardships every day' (p. 25). Similarly, Tjalaminu Mia shares stories of strong Aboriginal women who have influenced her life and her journey of reclaiming cultural heritage, overcoming racism and other colonial practices, and reconciling past hurts to establish proud and strong Aboriginal families:

> *I share the journey I made, which also includes my family stories. This highlights the importance of valuing our own cultural and social knowledge and oral histories. What I have learned over time through my mother's voice – our stories are our history, and our history, our country – are fundamental lessons for us, as individuals and cultural communities. The responsibility is ours, as individuals and as a group, to reinforce this truth to our peoples and young ones as a positive goal, to reclaim our cultural ways.* (p. 43)

Overcoming the devastation of colonisation and building a better world for Aboriginal people is, without doubt, the agenda of each of the authors. The various chapters prompt many questions, including matters related to Aboriginal women's leadership roles, collective and individual responsibilities, obligations and rewards, and gendered and broader community needs and benefits. As Aboriginal women we should share our feelings, our views and our ideas. We should recognise and be generous of our frailties as well as our strengths. We are human; we succeed and excel, we make mistakes, and sometimes have arguments and disagree. These are all aspects of who we are and this book celebrates who we are as Aboriginal women, our journeys, our experiences, influences, truths and worldviews.

In her chapter MaryAnn Bin-Sallik explains that her agenda is to tell 'my truth, and the consequences of my truth that have shaped and moulded my life' (p. 57). MaryAnn reflects on and shares the truth of her life experiences – childhood influences, her growing sociopolitical awareness in her teenage years and her training as a nurse and later as an academic. MaryAnn analyses these childhood activities, events and understanding through the lens of her adult self: prominent Aboriginal educator, experienced academic, humanitarian and global citizen.

Several of the authors have taken on this form of self-reflection and analysis in their respective chapters. Joan Winch writes a reflective piece that briefly covers her childhood and the government policies that affected her family, her early experiences in her chosen profession of nursing and her experiences of racism and sexism. Joan's story will resonate with many Aboriginal women and most importantly highlights her empowered, positive and proactive response to injustices facing Aboriginal people.

Jeannie Herbert contemplates how and who she has become by asking 'identity – who am I? – and representation – what do I stand for?' (p. 81). Other reflections include an identification of who she is now and her worldview, and those intellectual traditions that have shaped her. The latter includes an acknowledgement of the centrality of lessons learned from female relatives – mother and grandmother. Jeannie concludes her chapter by saying,

> *It is the intellectual traditions and learning experiences I have acquired through my life that have enabled me to know who I am as an Aboriginal woman, thus enabling the 'real' me to stand up when needed.* (p. 94)

We women play vital roles within our families and communities and we always need to be mindful of what we are doing to further the issues and priorities of Aboriginal women as well as further the issues of the Aboriginal community. A lot of what women do often goes unrecognised or unnoticed because they work behind the scenes and do not always push themselves forward. This work should be acknowledged, recognised and celebrated.

Ambelin Kwaymullina writes about the storytelling traditions of Indigenous women, a tradition that continues to this day and encompasses creation stories as well as the more recent stories within our communities 'of death, dispossession and destruction' (p. 100). This elegant chapter blends the past, present and future – drawing on the intellectual traditions of Indigenous women, telling their stories of dispossession, and their stories as creators of the future. Ambelin poses the question that many Indigenous people, including the editors of this book, struggle with:

> *What stories can we as women now tell to ourselves and to our children that will enable us to value our holistic Indigenous selves? That will equip us to perceive and sustain the connections between people and people, and people and country, which have always been the core of an Indigenous way of being? And that have allowed us to so far overcome the devastation of*

> *colonisation so that we can imagine the possibility of a better world for ourselves and for future generations of Indigenous people?* (p. 100)

A question that arose during the production of this book was 'Who are our role models?' To a large degree the Aboriginal women we see as role models are women who work hard for our communities and are not recognised necessarily as big leaders. We see them working hard, we see Aboriginal women being dedicated, we see our mums and our aunties working behind the scenes doing a lot just to keep families together, to keep communities together. We have had grandmas looking after all the kids and we have got women who are struggling and fighting to get things done, particularly in their local communities. There are many examples throughout Australia of strong Aboriginal female role models who have made significant achievements that have created space for others, like many of the authors in this book, to step forward and build on these achievements. And while these achievements have been made by individual women, many of us feel it is harder for Aboriginal women to step forward as individuals and that our preference would be to step forward with one or more of our sisters, as in doing so there are shared benefits as well as affirmation of collective responsibilities and obligations. The notion of role models, leading the way, breaking new ground and walking alone, of resistance and resilience are further themes running through many of the chapters in this book.

Pat Dudgeon tells the story of her grandmother and great-grandmother. This story of resistance, resilience and victory over adversity is very skilfully grounded in time and place, framed within a vivid sociopolitical context that gives the reader a clear insight into the strength and dogged independence of her foremothers. This chapter is about Indigenous women's views of identity, sexuality and gender, and the dialogue is woven around and through the story of Martha and Lillian. Pat explains the importance of such stories:

> *Through their stories and ours, we can name oppressions and injustices, we can name our strengths, culture and spirituality, and we can also celebrate how we as individuals had to, and still do, join together to make rich lives amid the difficulties.* (p. 109).

Many of the authors would agree that as Aboriginal women we want to put forward an Aboriginal women's agenda, not only an Aboriginal community agenda. We want to highlight those things that matter to Aboriginal women, that are based on our gendered knowledge, our understandings of the world and our perceptions of how we think the world could be better – and that is the defining point about Aboriginal women in leadership. If we are putting forward an Aboriginal women's agenda and are representing Aboriginal women then we have to talk to other Aboriginal women and get feedback and support from them. Several authors write about their leadership experiences. Those of us in leadership positions believe we have an obligation to genuinely attempt to represent Aboriginal interests in whatever sphere we are working within, not just to maintain the status quo or just agree with the dominant Western thinking. Putting forward a broad Aboriginal agenda looks after country, family and community.

Irene Watson, drawing from her work *Law-full Women*, examines and grapples with 'truth' and 'the one true story', how this can be represented without being captured by the colonial project, and the author's role and authority in the telling of the story. Irene urges Aboriginal women to tell 'the one true story' as it will 'amplify the marginal voices of First Nations' (p. 133) and reveal knowledge 'that does not impose itself but informs our world' in 'working towards a better empowered, decolonised Aboriginal space' (p. 134).

Nerida Blair focuses on her journey of finding her voice as an Indigenous scholar as well as finding a space, a language and a model that enables a truer representation of Indigenous knowing. A key point in Ned's journey of 'intellectual self-determination' was being introduced to mind mapping, which she considers a very appropriate tool of Indigenous expression. Ned states that,

> *Mind maps were created with a belief that these would reflect more of the brain functioning as a holistic process – linear and non-linear ... mind maps can serve as a bridge that enables validation of our experiences of Indigenous Knowings.* (p. 150)

Her journey led her to develop an Indigenous research methodology grounded by and centred around Indigenous Knowings which can 'interact with Western knowledges in critical and discerning ways' (p. 155).

Sandy O'Sullivan writes about the Aboriginal lesbian experience and points out that while there is a growing body of knowledge on Aboriginal women's identity issues, there continues to be very little written on Aboriginal lesbians. Sandy analyses discourses of Aboriginal gender representations and identity markers (such as the United Nations markers) to ascertain their ability to adequately frame and reflect the experiences and identity of Aboriginal lesbians. Sandy obviously hopes that other Aboriginal lesbians will write and share their ideas and experiences of what defines them and what constitutes their identity,

> *I share many moments with my straight Aboriginal sisters, but there are as many moments of divergence as convergence, and our communities are stronger for that diversity and richness of difference.* (p. 170)

As Black Women Do by Vanessa Lee captures the ongoing strength and resilience of Indigenous women in the face of adversity, including social class structures that discriminate against Indigenous women and consign them to the lower socio-economic ranks within Australia. Vanessa speaks to the holistic worldview of Indigenous women and how Indigenous gendered knowledges are taught that prepare Indigenous women to cope with life experiences and challenges,

> *This women's lore begins at a very young age and continues through the lifespan, preparing women with an understanding of how to cope with stressful situations in today's society.* (p. 217)

While each contributor clearly has her own areas of interest and expertise, and does different things in different areas, we are all engaged in putting forward a broad educational agenda, one that is sometimes gendered and at other times for the benefit of all Aboriginal people. For example, Dawn Bessarab explores Aboriginal women's views on gender and writes about gender formation and the intersection of race and class. Dawn shows that Aboriginal women's experiences of gender and formation of their gender identities is influenced by Aboriginal kinship relationships, Aboriginality, female and male relatives, Aboriginal and non-Aboriginal institutions and communities as well as family and individual economic status. Likewise Lyn Henderson-Yates examines an area that is of interest to the broader Aboriginal community in her investigation of the intersection between whiteness and Aboriginality through issues of identity questioning; the motivations of the questioners; the concept and enactments of whiteness; Aboriginal identity conception and formation; the invisibility of fair-complexioned Aboriginal people; and subject positions. Within this intersection, Lyn generously reflects on her lived experience and shares some of her life story about her Aboriginal self, and uses these experiences to engage in a critical analysis of how and why non-Aboriginal people attempt to define and impose identities on Aboriginal people.

In this book we share with you the thoughts and reflections of fifteen Aboriginal women on matters of significance and importance to us. For the editors, the importance of this venture was to talk about and bring together a community of women who, throughout their lives, have striven to enhance the lives of their people and communities. We have engaged in a dialogue about women's knowledge, about gendered and community positions and about our intellectual traditions. The agendas we put forward come from our life experiences and consider the needs of the broader Aboriginal community as well as those of Aboriginal women.

This writing project we women embarked on was ambitious but we have succeeded in reaching our goal. Collections such as this, written solely by Aboriginal women, are scarce in Australia and are vitally important as they provide unique insights into our lives. Aboriginal women's voices have been silenced in many ways during the processes of colonisation. We will be silent no longer.

MARY TERSZAK (Woods) is a Nyoongah from the South West of Western Australia and resides in East Maitland, New South Wales. Mary has two children and two grannies and frequently travels back to her country. She has published her book, *Orphaned by the Colour of My Skin*, in 2008. Mary is a PhD student at the Centre for Aboriginal Studies, Curtin University, and is currently working on a collection of stories about the Stolen Generations. She occasionally works as an Aboriginal mentor for Metford Public School.

SEPARATED IN 1944

Mary Terszak

In 1905 the Aborigines Act was implemented in Western Australia. This legislated that 'mixed blood' Aboriginal children would be removed from their families to be encouraged to grow up white. Western Australia reinforced this draconian legislation with the 1936 Native Administration Act. I was born in 1942 and was directly subjected to these policies. In 1944, I was with my mother at Carrolup Mission in the South West of Western Australia when I was removed from her and placed into Sister Kate's Home in Queens Park, a suburb of Perth. I was two years of age and I grew up with the understanding that I was an orphan, away from my family. In 2008, the then Prime Minister, Kevin Rudd, issued a historic Apology to Indigenous Australians for the period of time the government removed Aboriginal children from their families. The tragic consequences of this policy are still a part of Indigenous Australian history and experience. This chapter provides an insight into my story as a member of the Stolen Generations. Being removed meant that we grew up without family surroundings and, importantly, mothering. As an Aboriginal woman, my own mothering role is central to my sense of self. I reflect here upon the loss of my own mother and what that has meant for me.

My connection to my daughter as her 'mum' is wonderful as we have shared so much together throughout the years. We are best friends; we laugh at the silliest things and remember lots of fabulous moments. Yet, we also cry together. At least we have this – the lifetime of our shared experiences, her growing up with me, my love and protection of her and hers for me, getting to know her as a human being and our strong, unbreakable bond as mother and daughter. I was denied the opportunity to do this with my own mother.

My daughter calls me 'Lady' or 'Nanny Noo' and these nicknames are so precious to me. My son refers to me as 'Honey' and often thanks me for being his 'mum and dad' because I played both roles for my children. So I guess I have touched the hearts of my children in a special way. I am their mum. The word 'mum' is special for me and I treasure the term when my children use it. It has particular significance as I was never able to use it myself. I was never able to call someone mother.

As babies we are all born to a mother and father and without parents to start our lives, we would not exist. We are supposed to be born into a family and the child who has been is blessed to have a home with parents to take care of them. When a child grows and begins to speak, one of the first words they may say is 'mum' or 'dad', which is the most joyful and profound sound a parent might hear for the very first time. Unfortunately, this was not a reality for me for I am a product of the assimilation policies that were implemented right around Australia. So many Aboriginal children who, like me, were removed from their parents were similarly denied the opportunity to name their parents 'mum' or 'dad'.

In 1989 I finally met my birth mother but I could not bring myself to call her 'mum'. My mother's name is Elizabeth Clare Woods (nee Khan) and I call her 'Old Girl' as I cannot bring myself to say 'mother' or 'mum' because it doesn't feel right. When I first met her, I was in shock and felt my whole self crumble when I realised this little woman with her leg in plaster and wearing sunglasses was actually my biological mother. My excitement to finally meet her after decades of not having a mother suddenly went away. The expectations of this meeting were totally different to the reality; this reality was not what I imagined. My happiness turned into disappointment and I was overwhelmed with feeling this and blame for my mother. Many people might not understand this but they haven't had my experience, they haven't walked my journey, felt my sadness, despair, rejection and hate as a child and the confusion about why she didn't stay with me. Today, as an adult, I know the truth of our colonial history and I realise that there was nothing my mother could have done to fight the system.

I visit Perth regularly for my studies and I try to visit Old Girl at Belmont. It is sad to see this frail, thin, little Aboriginal woman with no teeth, with shoes and socks on, a summer dress and jumper, grey hair in a middle part and the back tied in a ponytail. Every time I go to see her, she is sitting on a single lounge chair towards the end of the room watching Channel 10 on the television. In wintertime the wood fire is burning and her little dog is sitting not too far away from her. I suppose she is happy with the warmth of her home but I wonder when she is sitting all alone if she ever thinks, does she ever wonder, where her lost child is. That little girl never returned, but a grown woman – a mother with her own two children – arrived as a complete stranger 50 years later.

The little old woman who I call Old Girl is 83 years of age. The child in me imagines how wonderful it would be if she were to reach out to me with a hug and say: 'I am your 'mum' and you are home at last.' But the distance of time is too great, the space between us is impossible to cross because, as a 65 year old, I cannot turn back time for the two-year-old Nyoongah child within me who still feels an unmet urge for her mother to hold her. I yearn for the bonds and feeling of belonging that others take for granted in their everyday family lives.

I have never been able to say with genuine feeling of love the word 'mum'. I was taken from my people and placed into an institution that was dedicated to changing me, that transformed me into an entirely different person. The Nyoongah child within me is still suffering with the loss of a mother and sometimes cannot handle the everyday situations that arise. There is this yearning to belong and the child cannot always cope as the adult wants life to change to overcome the emotional trauma of the past 64 years. I constantly wonder why there was an assimilation policy in this country, a policy that destroyed the most important relationship any child could possibly have in a lifetime – with their mother and family.

In 2007 I was talking with another 'home kid' about how nobody cared about me while I was in the home for 18 years, when she surprised me by responding 'Woodsie'. I remembered when we used to hold hands and go off to kindergarten together. We were only four years of age. Her words evoked memories of the love and comfort that we children had shared in the home. I cherish this moment of happiness and innocence and in my mind's eye still see us holding hands. The simplest things that we take for granted, like holding hands with our grannies (grandchildren) and other family members, are precious.

I am grateful that this has never happened to my family, to the two children that I am very proud of and who call me 'mum'. It is beautiful, because you belong to others who are a part of you. I appreciate how wonderful this is and what an amazing gift of life I have produced in birth. I am sad that my children never had the chance to have their 'nanny' and this makes me 'wild' knowing that they have missed out on something special. A nanny plays a huge role in a child's life and even further into adulthood. My grannies have been blessed with a nanny (me), an uncle and of course their mum and dad. I have played a major role in my grannies' lives, being able to support my daughter when they were only babies. I had many nights without sleep and that is okay, because my love for these two grannies is immense. They come to nanny's house and nanny can stay at their place, and we develop our family in a loving and healthy way. My daughter often asks me to have a 'sleepover' and I laugh as I live only four streets away from her. I appreciate that we can have this family togetherness in such a special way.

In the home there were 'housemothers' and I never understood why they were called this because there was no mothering. It was merely a title given by those in charge to identify these women as the head of the cottage. The housemothers that I had in my 18 years never meant anything to me and they could never come close to being a substitute for a 'mum'.

I think of Old Girl and how she must have felt the day they took me away from her. A mother at 19 years of age having her life all turned upside down. One minute having a daughter and then nothing at all. She was already a single parent and I cannot imagine the devastation she must have felt on that dreadful day of separation. I have a memory of myself at four years old screaming and holding tightly onto another home girl's dress when she was trying to leave. The memory of the fear stays with me. I have wondered if this was from an earlier memory, perhaps when I was taken from my mother.

I have started to work with Old Girl on her life story; we talk and I tape her and write up the discussions. Listening to her voice and hearing about the tragic things she speaks of in her life story makes me sad. At moments like this I search within myself for the strength to look at things differently and accept this little old lady for who she is. Life has been unfair and the damage to my soul and hers is terrible. I will learn to accept and forgive, and perhaps one day I will call her 'mum'. As a very angry child and an insecure adult in my times of pain, sadness and rejection, I would have loved to have gone home to my 'mum', laid my head on her shoulder and cried about how I was feeling. I think that just to be nurtured in my mother's arms for only five minutes would have given me a sense of security.

There are Aboriginal people who don't believe that the Apology is important to us. Every individual makes their own decisions and determines what is right for them. In my case the Apology, the act of saying sorry, is very important and I am in touch with a number of people from similar situations who feel the same. As adults, at last we have the right to make our own decisions because we are no longer the children of Sister Kate's Home who had to agree with everything that one person in authority said. It is not easy for people of the Stolen Generations to feel comfortable speaking about a 'mum' because we never grew up with this special word.

It took this Australia a long time to accept and recognise Aboriginal people for who they are and to finally apologise to the Stolen Generations. I stood with a diversity of Aboriginal people in Canberra and revelled in this most historic day. This is a moment that we will never forget, but unfortunately it didn't take away the suffering of a mother and daughter who will continue to carry the hurt and grief of their separation. The Apology did not break down the barriers for this child to be able to say 'mum' openly and freely to the world. It will never give my children their 'nanny' or my granddaughters their great-grandmother, but it validates the history and the pain that was caused. It gives hope that, in the future, nothing like this will happen again.

To survive as an Aboriginal woman I needed to look at what was important in my life. Much of my personal journey has involved reclaiming my cultural background – both the similarities and differences within this, my extended family – and negotiating a comfortable self that includes my lived experiences as a person from the Stolen Generations. From childhood experience I needed to be more than a mother; I had to overcome many personal barriers to be a good, decent, loving person. I found strength and the determination to begin a healing process. My journey involved support and love from many people and without that support, I may not have survived spiritually. I know many others who came from the home who did not survive. I feel that having hope is important and that Aboriginal people have hope and we have to learn to reach out to support each other. I am a stronger person as a result of my quest to reclaim my own sense of self and Nyoongah identity after being caught up in the assimilation policies of the past.

DR CHERYL KICKETT-TUCKER (PhD, MS, BAppSc, AssDipAppSc) is from the Wadjuk, Ballardong and Yued peoples in Western Australia. She has worked with Aboriginal people all her life in the fields of education, sport and health. Cheryl is a Research Fellow at Telethon Institute for Child Health Research and is Principal of Koya Indigenous Research Group, an independent and Aboriginal-owned organisation. She completed her PhD and post-doctoral studies exploring the sense of self, identity, culture and self-esteem of urban Aboriginal children.

SHIRLEY HARRIS is a Wadjuk woman from Western Australia. She is retired but worked most of her life for Aboriginal people in aged care, hospitals and shelters. Later she worked in the former federal Department of Aboriginal Affairs and the Western Australian Department of Health. She is currently an artist who paints Noongar stories passed down to her from her parents. Shirley has written many Noongar stories to accompany her art and this is the first published piece.

Shirley Harris, Cheryl Kickett-Tucker and her daughter Sarah. Courtesy the author

Artwork opposite page by Shirley Harris

WIND SPIRIT: NANNA'S LEGACY

Cheryl Kickett-Tucker and Shirley Harris

Ever since I can remember, my Mother, Shirley Harris, has been painting. Her art depicts her passion, thoughts and attitudes of Noongar stories as well as her own personal ideas. For most of my adult life, Mum has always painted me a story for my birthday. The last couple of years, the story has been the same theme and the artwork has been colourful, vibrant, moving and strong. This latest series of works I have been fortunate to receive is called *Wind Spirits*. For me, these pieces represent and tell about the strength and spirit of Aboriginal women and how we must remain strong, reliable and responsible despite being challenged with life's hardships every day. As portrayed in the paintings, we guard our home (nest) and the children who occupy it, but as we carry out this role, the wind (life's circumstances) is constantly at our door. The wind moves and shapes us each and every day. Sometimes the wind is hard and fast and comes from all directions, and at other times it is soft and sweet like a cool breeze on a hot summer night. Even knowing the force of the wind and the challenges it brings, we remain focused, stable, reliable and responsible for the sake of our home and all the children, grandchildren, nieces, nephews, fostered children, adopted children and extended kin who may come and go over our lifetime. Sometimes the wind may push us where we haven't been before, but we always have our spirit to guide us along the challenging and unpredictable corridors of life. Our spirit keeps us determined, focused, solid – moorditj (Noongar word for solid, strong, healthy). As Aboriginal women and Mothers, we pass on our spirit to younger women. We share our skills, knowledge and history of who we are, what we stand for, what is important, our morals, integrity and, of course, the meaning of love. We pass on a legacy. I often reflect and wonder about the lives of the strong, moorditj Mothers, of whom I am a descendant, and the path set before me as a Mother. I ponder the potential influence of my moorditj Mothers' legacies for me in raising my daughters. For instance, how did my grandmother's legacy affect my Mother? How has my Mother's legacy affected me? I am writing this story from the perspective of a yorga (woman) and ngangk (Mother), but guided by the lived experiences, wisdom and integrity of my Mother as she shares her Mother's story with me.

I am from the South West of Western Australia and I have lived all of my life between the Derbal Yerrigan (Swan River) and Moorda (Darling Scarp), which are in my traditional Wadjuk country. My family are also from the wheatbelt areas near Perth and I am a very proud Wadjuk, Balladong and Yued yorga. I have been married for 22 years to a Wongi man of the Goldfields of Western Australia. We have been blessed with three wonderful children. My Mother is Shirley Harris and my father is Allan Kickett and I have been fortunate to come from a large family of three brothers and four sisters. I interviewed my Mother to develop this story and I begin with the Aboriginal custom associated with naming a child, because the names we give our children are a step towards forging a moorditj ngangk's legacy.

After my husband and I named our first child Jaylon, we were faced with the rules of Aboriginal naming customs and the cultural obligation that we are expected to uphold. Aboriginal naming customs are passed from family to family and from Mother to Mother. Although acknowledging and respecting the naming customs, my husband and I wanted to give our first-born son a unique and distinctive name. We named him Jaylon, which means 'victorious' and 'swift bird, like an eagle'. Jaylon made us proud parents the day he breathed life on Mother earth and, like the eagle, he was born strong, healthy and extremely alert. Some of my kin were not happy with his name. Being a first-time Mother, my postnatal hormones went crazy and so I was easily distressed by their dissatisfaction. My husband and I remained determined despite many tears and much frustration. I couldn't be happier because today my son is a tall, handsome, strong and compassionate 21 year old with a unique character that is befitting of his distinctive name.

When my second child was born, my husband and I (particularly me) were well aware of the naming customs, given our experiences with our first born. Our second child is Sarah, a beautiful, kind and compassionate 16 year old. She was named after six grandmothers. Sarah means 'princess' and 'pure' and she is so named after her great-great-great-great-grandmother Sarah Ryder, whose Noongar name was Bunderan, and her great-great-great-grandmother Sarah Jane Kickett. My Mother often calls my Sarah, Sarah Jane, yet her middle name is Katelyn. Her middle name is a compilation of four grandmothers where 'Kate' refers to her great-great-grandmother Catherine Ryder (nee Egan), her great-grandmother Kathleen Harris (nee Ryder) and her grandmother Kathleen Tucker (nee Barnes). 'Lyn' refers to Linda Barnes (nee Smith), who is Sarah's great-grandmother. The reason we named our girl after our grandmothers was because Sarah's name is befitting of her and because of our obligation to the naming customs. Sarah is a strong-willed child who is extremely determined to be herself and to get her own way. On her softer side, she is a social character who loves to interact and 'yarn' with everyone. She has an extremely affectionate nature and is very considerate of others. A name has great importance. In Sarah's case, we named her so because of the little spark we saw when she was born, but she is also named out of respect for her grandmothers and the legacy they have forged.

Ten years had passed when our second daughter arrived. She is Caris Tia Byuwara, a dark-haired beauty just like her older sister. Caris means 'my lovely, my beloved'. Tia is translated to 'princess' and Byuwara is her paternal great-great-grandmother's name. Similar to the story of Molly in *Rabbit Proof Fence*, Byuwara walked over 1000 kilometres back home from Moore River Settlement to the northeastern Goldfields. So Caris is my beloved and lovely princess, while Sarah is my pure princess and Jay is my swift bird. The following is my story of the legacy forged by my moorditj Mothers ... my

Nanna, Kathleen Harris (nee Ryder), my Mother, Shirley Harris, myself and my daughters, Sarah and Caris.

I didn't meet my grandmother, Kathleen, because she passed away in 1960, eight years before I was born. In fact, none of my seven siblings met Nan. I've always wondered about my grandparents, our family history, and have felt a strong desire to know more about my family, especially my Mother's Mother. I never knew much about my Nanna but I have always felt a strong connection to her. Being an extremely sentimental person, I often take things to heart and family are closest to my heart than anything else in this world. When the time was appropriate and I felt strong emotionally, I engaged in a series of very long yarns with my Mother to learn more. Mum told me many things, sad things but mostly happy things about her life as a child and about her Mother. I found that I have a very strong connection to my Nanna, despite not meeting her. This is what I learned ...

Kathleen Rosina Ryder was born 23 March 1910, a birth date we share. Rosina was her baptised name, but not her registered middle name. She was born at Koojong Station, near Moora, in Western Australia's Wheatbelt region. Koojong was owned by the Padbury family. In fact, they owned vast amounts of land around Moora and Guildford. Nan's parents were William Ryder (son of Walter Padbury, former mayor of Guildford) and Catherine Egan. They had nine children and Nan was the youngest. My great-grandparents lived in a mud house. It was number four at New Norcia Mission near Moora. The 1905 Aborigines Act, which appointed Chief Protector AO Neville as the legal guardian of all Aboriginal people, ensured my Nan was placed in the care of Spanish missionaries in New Norcia and she grew up there at 'Girls Town', a three-storey dormitory for Aboriginal girls.

Nan stood 5 foot and 1 inch tall. She had beautiful, smooth, dark skin and matching dark brown eyes. Nan wore her straight, black hair just above her shoulders, with a right side part that was pinned into a curl behind her small ears. She possessed an easy-going nature, but was straight to the point and made her true thoughts and feelings known. Nan would say what was needed and then leave it at that. She never, ever held grudges with anyone. Nan was a good person who loved music and dancing. Blue was her favourite colour and each day she would try to wear something blue. She loved to wear a dust jacket which covered her whole body and lyle stockings. Nan and I share many similarities besides our birth date and star sign, Aries, because

Lyndon Charles Harris (Pop) and Kathleen Rosina Ryder (Nan) on their wedding day, 1931. Courtesy the author

my favourite colour is also blue and I love to wear blue more than any other colour. We both love the same perfume, Lily of the Valley, and the smell of roses. Nan loved wearing Ashes of Roses body powder and I often buy rose-perfumed talcum powder at Christmas time. Above all, there was one characteristic about my Nanna that everybody was familiar with: her love for her children. Nan may have been short in stature but the care she gave her children was larger than life itself. She loved her children so much and dedicated her whole self to them, a loving part of her being which I definitely have adopted.

When Nan was a teenager, she was working as a domestic house servant at Padbury's House in Guildford. She was upstairs dusting the curtains and looked out the window to see a strapping young Aboriginal man tending to horses. He was her future husband and my Pop, Lyndon Charles Harris. He was born in 1907 at Onslow to parents Edward William Harris and Alice Wilkes. Pop was the only son of four children. At the time he met my Nan, he was working for the Padbury family in Guildford and, according to Mum, they didn't really like each other on their first meeting. But with time, love conquered all and they were married at New Norcia Mission in 1931. Nan was 21 years of age. The wedding ceremony was performed entirely in Spanish. Her wedding bonnet and bouquet consisted of beautiful, spectacular orange blossoms with waxed leaves. She looked radiant and Pop was handsome in his smart-looking suit. They had ten children, of which my Mother is the fifth born, just as I am the fifth born in my family. Coincidently, I married Quinton, whose name means the fifth born also!

Nan and Pop shared a few homes in my traditional Wadjuk country. They lived on the reserve in Success Hill (an eastern suburb of Perth).

Success Hill was a place of significance to the Wadjuk people because of the Dreaming stories of the Waugal, the importance of the Bennet Brook spring, Derbal Yerrigan and because of the traditional ceremonies that took place. Today, on the same site where my Nan lived are my Mother's Noongar stories and paintings standing immortalised for all to see in a cultural-themed recreation park.

Pop and Nan then moved to a farm house in Beechboro near Charlie's shops (on Walter Road), which has been operating on the same site for over 40 years and is well known among the locals for its European foods, cakes and drinks. In about 1939 they moved from there to another Padbury property in Bayswater (another eastern suburb of Perth), where they had five children. Soon after moving there, tragedy struck the family because Nan's sister, Martha Ryder, passed away at a young age and left behind five children. Nan took them in and cared for them as part of the family. She grew up all children together as one. There were no distinctions about who cousins were and who siblings were. According to Mum, 'We were all brothers and sisters.' However, Aunty Martha's older three children left Nan's home in less than a year and Nan looked after the two younger children, Uncle Stanley and Uncle Charlie, until they were taken away to Clontarf Aboriginal Boys' Home. They both ran away from the Boys' Home and eventually found their way back to their family.

Nan and Pop lived on a farming property called Allan Brown's Dairy where there were two workers' houses on the property. The Harris family lived in the first house, which was a weatherboard home with a tin roof. The second house accommodated a Noongar family, the Parfitts. The front of Nan's house faced the western horizon (on the site of what is now Chisholm Catholic College in Bayswater) and the highest point that could be seen from the dairy was St Mary's Cathedral (near Royal Perth Hospital). Consequently, all of Nan's children were baptised there. The house had one bedroom at the front, a kitchen, lounge and another bedroom. It accommodated two adults and up to 10 children.

As well as the Parfitts, the other families living at Allan Brown's property were the Mippies, Bodneys and Brophos and all the children used to play together. Mum was about three at the time and she still remembers playing with the other children. Her eldest sister Freda was 10 years older and one day she made Mum a roller. It was made from a Sunshine powder milk tin and filled with sand. On each side of the tin was a hole where a wire passed through and joined outside the tin to form a handle. Attached to the handle was a piece of string which was used to pull the roller along. One day Nancy Parfitt (who was about the same age as Mum) saw the roller and cried for it and eventually was given the roller by adults. The roller belonged to Mum and so she started to cry to have it back. So 13-year-old Aunty Freda conjured up a plan to get the roller back from Nancy. Aunty Freda had to get Nancy's mind off the roller so she kept her occupied by talking to her. After a short while, Aunty Freda told her sister, Aunty Joan (then aged nine), to keep talking to Nancy, which she did and Aunty Freda went around the back of the house so that Nancy couldn't see her. She went up behind Nancy with a pair of scissors and cut the rope from the roller. Unbeknown to Nancy, the roller was quietly taken away and given back to its rightful owner, my Mum. Big sisters to the rescue! Nancy still had hold of the string and thought she still had the roller! Mum told me she had to keep the roller out of sight for a couple of days until Nancy forgot about it. The legacy of Nan's care was set and although her daughters were young, they were living the legacy already ... caring for each other, particularly looking after the young ones.

It was a hard life in Bayswater for Kathleen Harris and her young, growing family because my Pop spent large amounts of time away from them seeking his fortune in the Goldfields. There wasn't much work around the Bayswater area so he went panning for gold. Mum said that, 'He always had these ideas about striking it rich.' He prospected some 1100 kilometres northeast of Perth between Menzies, Pigwell and Leonora. During his prospecting days, Pop met mate and fellow prospector Sydney 'Snowy' Barnes, a Wongi man who just happens to be my children's great-grandfather. Snowy found gold at the infamous 'rabbit warren' north of Leonora. My Pop found a gold vein, but he never went back to the Goldfields to work it. According to Mum, he had everything prepared (including the dry blower, which pumps dry air to separate gold from the soil) but couldn't go back because he fell ill.

Nan didn't say much about life when Pop was absent from the young family, but rather she got on with what she had to do and rarely fussed. It was during this time between 1937 and 1940 that Nan lost two of her own children to sickness: a boy aged six months and a girl aged about three years. Mum recalled that, 'her brother died from cot death in Bassendean and sister died at Princess Margaret Hospital [PMH] in Subiaco from gastroenteritis.

When sister got sick, Mum and Dennis Anderson [Mum's relative] pushed her in a pram from Beechboro to Subiaco, some 12 kilometres by foot. She passed away in the little wooden house at the front of PMH. She was just three years old.'

Despite the grieving times that fell upon the family, Nan stood strong and her children gained their strength and compassion from the way in which Nan handled challenging incidents. She had ageless wisdom and was a pillar of support. Nan maintained her spirit in times of great sorrow, though she silently mourned the loss of her beloved little ones. Nan's strong spirit was called upon again when Pop arrived home at the family residence in Bayswater after a three-year absence. Nan broke the sad news to Pop about the loss of his beloved son and daughter. Mum said, 'Pop was a very loving father towards to his children and was devastated to lose his only son and young daughter.'

Years later, hard times came upon Nan once again when Pop suffered a stroke. Nan helped Pop overcome his stroke and nursed him back to health. She looked after the children's daily needs, kept them safe and secure, maintained a stable home and comforted their spirit with her strong and caring nature despite her own suffering. Mum reflected upon Nan and her source of strength during times of sorrow, grief, hardship, racism and other troubles and said that, 'Nan had a huge family support from the Ryders and I think that gave her the strength. She was one of these women who didn't complain about anything, but took everything on the chin and just did things. She was a strong person because she had to be strong ... and take on all the things that happened in those days. And sometimes, we didn't have tucker (food) but she'd always go out to find things to feed her family.'

According to my Mother, Pop never had much to do with the children's daily upbringing, but he was always there for the family at night. During the day, he followed his pursuits, but Nan never had any pursuits because her life and passion were dedicated to the wellbeing of her family and children. Mum said, 'Nan was just always home looking after us and always had time to be with us.' As well as other activities and events, Nan treated the children to regular, special outings to the theatre. She made sure she saved money for the movies and every Wednesday fortnight she and the children would go to the Civic Theatre in Inglewood. They walked about 3 miles to get there and 3 miles back. On Saturdays, however, they would catch the tram into Perth city to the Grand Theatre on Murray Street. There were 10 of them taking the trip to the city, the whole family (except Pop), and they took up all the seats in a single carriage. The conductor would say to Nan, 'You should get a tram for yourselves!' The Grand was famous for western movies and the likes of Gene Aultry, Roy Rogers, Hop-a-long Cassidy and Randolph Scott graced the golden screen. Mum remembers, 'We'd come out of there about half past seven, and we'd see all these women going up to the Unity Hall with all their big ball gowns on. We used to love that because of all the pretty dresses they used to have and I'd say, 'That's my dress!', and my sister would say, 'No, that's *my* dress!!' We would have a competition about which dress was the prettiest.'

When they arrived home after the movies, Nan would prepare a feast of delicacies – rollmops (a rollmop is a piece of raw fish dipped in vinegar with a skewer through it), green olives, fresh Italian bread and rabbit from the local shop – which everyone thoroughly enjoyed. Nan would then make a pan damper or bannick (as it is sometimes called) and these were often ladled with loads and loads of thick, sweet treacle or honey ... another delicacy!

Nan faced some difficult experiences with strangers in the street during these times. The 1905 Aborigines Act enforced a curfew which prohibited Aboriginal people to be in town after 6pm at night. Mum says that Nan was very dark skinned and it was because of her dark skin that she consistently experienced racism. When Nan got on the tram, the conductor frequently questioned her. If she was in town late, wedjulas (non-Aboriginal people) would tell her, 'You have to be out ... the curfew is on at six! You have to be out of this town area.' Mum recalled she was in town after curfew with Nan: 'I was about seven. We had to quickly rush to the bus and get on and get out of town before we were seen by the police. We were always pushed around. We did a lot of walking because the buses didn't go near our house, so we had to walk for miles when we got off the tram.'

Nan didn't have equal access to services like Pop. He wasn't scrutinised by the wider public to the same extent as his wife. Pop was light skinned and, according to Mum, he seemed to escape some of the racism. But one day an incident occurred with one of Pop's wedjula co-workers. They worked at Cresco in Bayswater and his co-worker kept racially abusing Pop for weeks on end, calling him names such as 'nigger'. Pop let him go, tolerating this day after day, until one day he put a stop to the abuse once and for all.

Pop challenged and fought the wedjula bloke and beat him thoroughly, putting an end to the matter.

My Mother, Shirley, reminded me that there were sad stories, but many happy stories and memories in our family history. She recalled a time when she and her sister Joanie had a pet chook. It was white, fat, old and extremely tame. The pet chook used to follow them everywhere, just like a dog. Mum and Aunty Joan used to wrap it up in a small blanket and tuck it into a doll's pram. The chook would stay put and Mum would place a baby's bonnet on its head which it tried to shake off. The bonnet, however, was firmly placed. The pet chook even used to sleep with Mum and Aunty Joan. One day it was walking around the garden and just keeled over dead. Mum said the chook became too fat, but I reckon it was spoiled with so much love from two little girls who knew first hand how to care for something smaller than themselves. The best teacher they could have had was my Nan. They placed the pet chook in a small wooden box and buried it at the back of the goona mia (toilet) near their tin house.

Nan's influence upon Mum was strong and obvious because Mum was just like Nan and looked after the younger ones. Uncle Kevin was a younger sibling who was extremely close to Mum. He was the only living son of Nan and Pop. One day, Uncle Kevin was given a little red truck to play with and every time he got mad, he would 'smash it up and bust it open'. The very next day Mum would put it back together because Uncle Kevin would be looking to play with it again and she didn't want him to be sad. Mum cared very much for her younger brother ... just like her Mother wanted her to do.

Nan was brought up as a Catholic and held extremely strong morals. She lived her life strictly adhering to these morals, which she passed on to her children. Mum said that she never slept past seven in the morning because Nan always had the children up early to clean and tidy the house immediately after breakfast. Nothing was out of place. Cleanliness and hygiene were important learnings for the children. Nan was a persistent teacher who taught her children to live by morals, always be respectful to elders and display appropriate behaviours.

Nan also taught her children Noongar ways with values which were respected and rules which were followed. She said that sweeping was not allowed at camp after sundown because it would wipe away the tracks of animals and people who visited the camp at night. Poking the coals in the main camp fire and making it spit so it sounded like a small firecracker was not allowed because it meant that a wirn (spirit of a person from the past) could be evoked to visit. Playing with firesticks at night was not permitted otherwise the child would wet the bed. Also forbidden was laughter at night because it brought winarch (bad luck). Whistling was especially not allowed at nightfall. This rule caused the children much fright because whistling invited the woordatj to the camp. The woordatj were described as little hairy men that could coax the children away from the camp and they would never be seen by their family again. The woordatj used sugar bags to take the children away and so any spare bags had to be folded at night and hidden out of sight. Mum recalled one night when she was being a little cheeky to Nan and asked, 'How they going to put me in there?' Nan retorted, 'Don't you worry, they are magic people and when they touch you they make you shrink [to put you in the sugar bag] and then they touch you again to make you big [when you are out].' Consequently, the woordatj was a feared being and the story kept the children close to the camp at night. The children were not allowed to break the balga (grass tree) spears because it meant that rain would come the next day, but Mum said this rule was really about protecting the environment, because the balga spears contained seed ready for the next season. Nan showed Mum how to find water in the balga, look for food and catch and prepare meat for consumption, including yonga (kangaroo), waitch (emu), ninyarn (echidna), yoorn (bobtail), doornart (twenty-eight parrot), jilgies (marron), yerderap (duck) and rabbit. Nan taught Mum many things about the bush and the Noongar way of life. She passed to her children much of her knowledge and skill about the land, seasons, culture, animals and people. Mum recalls that, 'We were brought up with a mixture of Noongar culture, white Australian culture, some English and Spanish, Irish ... even the food was of Spanish, Irish and Italian influences.' My Mum also passes on her knowledge through her oral stories and her paintings to enrich the lives of her children.

Nan was an educated person who wanted her children to read and write. When the family was living in the tin house in Bayswater, she enrolled Mum and Aunty Joan in St Peter's Catholic School in Inglewood. Mum was about six at the time. She and Joan had to walk a couple of miles to reach the school, so Nan would give Mum five pennies to buy a half loaf of bread and a penny worth of polony for their lunch. Mum said, 'On the way to school I would eat the centre out of the bread and then on the way home, I would eat the crust.' When the family moved to the bush along Albany Highway, Nan organised correspondence lessons for Mum, Uncle Kevin and Aunty Joan. Their 'formal education' continued in the bush and lessons were sent out in a paper roll. Lessons comprised English and maths as well as story-writing activities and Mum had two weeks to complete the tasks and send her work back. My Mother continued her education at Curtin University and has almost completed a Bachelor of Arts, majoring in English and Australian studies.

Sadly, in 1960 Kathleen Harris passed away from a treatable ailment at the age of 50 years. Mum was only 19 at the time. Nan's passing was a huge loss for our family and particularly for my Mother, who said that when Nan passed on, she lost her best friend. I couldn't contain my emotion when Mum shared her story and together we broke down in tears. I think it was the first time Mum had the opportunity to disclose this story and express her feelings with anyone. It was extremely powerful and took great courage and for that I am grateful, because I can now share Nan's story with my own daughter, Sarah, whom she is named after. After listening to Nan's story, I know that I am just like Kathleen Harris and that we share not only the same birth date but the same spirit as well. She left a legacy that showed me how to love my children and take care of my family. Kathleen Harris was patient, kind, compassionate and cared deeply, not only with her children but with others as well. Nan embraced all her learnings as a young person and shared it all with her children. She was an active and patient teacher who valued every moment with her children. Mum says that Nan was a good friend who was always there, never looked down on anyone, never said no to anyone and would 'give someone the coat off her back and the food off her plate'. In return, her children never disappointed her. This was her legacy to us.

My moorditj ngangk's legacy had journeyed from Mother to Mother. My Mum worked all her life for Aboriginal people in the Western Australian Department of Health and the former federal Department of Aboriginal Affairs (DAA). She juggled her home duties with full-time work and university studies. Mum was one of a small team of Aboriginal women at DAA who worked at a mid-management level. She made her way to management level after starting her employment at DAA as a clerical assistant, a feat that we are all proud of. Mum cared for us with the same intensity and love as Nan had cared for her. I can clearly see that Mum is a mirror image of her Mother and just as Nan had been there for her children, so too was my Mum there for all of us. She raised her eight children in very tough times and always made sure we had food in our belly, a warm bed and someone to talk to. Mum has always given to others, even the food off her plate. When I was about seven years of age my parents and seven siblings lived in Lockridge. We had a five-bedroom house with two bathrooms and two toilets. The house may have been a lot different to Nan's tin home in Bayswater, but my Mother still carried on the love for children as her Mother did. Mum cared for many others in our extended family too, like my cousins, my uncles and aunts. At any one time, up to 15 children resided with us. We had to share our beds and I remember sleeping in a small bunk bed with my sister Jocelyn. We slept head to toe so we could fit, but that meant smelling her toes all night! Mum also respected Nan's last wishes to look after her younger siblings and Uncle Stanley and Uncle Kevin were always with us.

Just like her Mother, Shirley Harris valued education and always ensured we went to school, cousins and all. There is no limit to helping others. Mum is a kind, compassionate and loving person who has done her Mother proud by raising her own children with the strong morals, values and respect that she was taught. Each of us are better people because of her love and the legacy she has taken up and passed on.

After reflecting upon my own life as a young, working Mother of three, I know that when things get tough, I can remember my Nanna, Kathleen Harris. I am assured of her strength, love, kindness, humility and compassion to get me through. If my memory fails me and I need reminding of her wonderful qualities, then I can look at my Mother, Shirley, for living proof. My success as a person, woman, Mother, friend, aunt and wife is only possible because of the struggles and experiences my Mother and grandmother have endured. I know that there is no way I would be here without the legacy of love towards a child forged by Nan and left for my Mum, who in turn has passed it to me. I have two young daughters and a son and I love them with every part of my being. I have taught them strong morals and respect for themselves, for others and for their Noongar and Wongi identities. I listen and we talk together. We share a very close bond as parent and child and I told my children that even as they get old and hairy, that I expect them to always give me and their Dad a cuddle and kiss ... no matter what age! I love to be with them each and every day and share as many experiences as I can with them. My children are my delight, pride and joy and I feel overwhelmingly blessed to be their Mother. Consequently, I live each day by ensuring my children are loved and I am there for them always, especially when the wind blows and challenges us as a family.

What's a legacy? It begins with the name we give our children. My Mother named me after her because as she said, 'I wanted one of my children to be like me.' Her name, Shirley Dawn, means 'from the meadow' and 'awakening of the dawn' and my name, Cheryl Susanne, is a French version of her name meaning 'dear one' and 'graceful lily'. Mum's baptised name, Catherine, and my daughter's middle name, Katelyn, are variations of my Nanna's Christian name. And I know that my Nanna was named with purpose because her names mean 'pure, innocent' (Kathleen) and a 'noted protector' (Rosina). So, we are all connected not only by birth and blood but also by the name which is given to us upon birth. Our legacy and spirit are intertwined with our names. Now when I look at my Mother's paintings, I see my Nanna encapsulated as the Wind Spirit, the strong person who may be tossed by winds of challenge and change, but who remains strong, reliable and responsible ... she truly was a 'noted protector' and has set the path for us to follow.

If, as Aboriginal Mothers and women, we find ourselves being challenged by daily winds and strong gales, then we need to search out our legacy. As portrayed in my Mother's paintings, let your wind spirits (from your Mothers) guide you through the challenges the wind may bring over your lifetime. An important source of strength lies within the stories of your Mothers, grandmothers, aunts, sisters, grandmothers' sisters, cousins and elders. Talk to your family and extended kin, know your history, appreciate their lives. Find your story because knowing it is a key to your legacy and when the gales of pain and trouble blow your way, you can count on your legacy to give you spirit and strength. If, for various reasons, you cannot locate your family or there are other roadblocks in your way, then speak with your paternal family, like your father's Mother, sisters and aunts. There is always a way to explore and uncover your legacy. Let your desire and passion drive you. Sometimes you may not see it at first, but stay focused, listen intently to your family's stories, close your eyes and *your story ... your legacy* will eventually reveal itself. When you find it, ask yourself how your legacy can help you in your life's journey as a person, woman, Mother and friend. I have started you off by sharing my legacy – my Nanna's Wind Spirit – with you. Show your children your love, goodness and strength. Keep them close and take time to really be with them. Love your children like my Nan did, like my Mother does and like I am doing now. Be kind and be patient and you won't be disappointed.

TJALAMINU MIA is a Menang, Goreng and Wardji woman of the Nyungar Nation, the Great Southern region of Western Australia. She was awarded the WA NAIDOC Community Person of the Year in 2012 and is a Stolen Generations survivor. She has worked in many government and community grassroots organisations, and was an Oral History, Culture and the Arts research fellow in the School of Indigenous Studies at the University of Western Australia. Tjalaminu is a published author and is currently Managing Director of the Sister Kate's Home Kids Healing Centre; she develops and delivers cultural healing programs for Sister Kate's Home Kids and their descendants, as well as other Stolen Generations groups and the wider Aboriginal community.

DESPERATELY SEEKING EMILY

Tjalaminu Mia

lost
alone
I am searching
Old woman
I need your touch

The years you kids were away from me and your grandparents caused us much heartache. We thought you would forget us and the family who loved you. It's good to see the work you're doing. Keep asking questions about our Old People, because they will not be forgotten and this will bring them closer if you need to feel secure in who you are.

Beryl Dixon

Though these words from my mother mean a lot to me, there are times on the most confident days I still freeze occasionally with inadequacies. There is now more space between these times, but when they do appear I draw on these words to help combat any misgivings I might be feeling. Although these words provide stability and a sense of belonging, for years many Aboriginal people like myself did not really know this and we lacked the understanding of what it meant at a deep level. This limited our ability to express ourselves in a culturally meaningful and family loving way, due to being a part of a group of people who experienced a 'mass identity crisis' not of our choosing. This came from the Western Australian government controlling Aboriginal people over the generations, under strict guidelines within legislation such as the 1905 Aborigines Act, 1936 Native Administration Act and the 1944 Citizens Rights Act.

Though I am of an age now where I am seen more as an older person, I often wonder how do we, parents of mission and reserve life, babies of the assimilation policies and children's homes, express ourselves and help our children to express themselves culturally in the society we live in today. Aboriginal people are becoming more aware of the difference of the dominant society's attitude over time: first of tolerance by people who saw themselves as superior and we as inferior, then intolerance and indifference by people who wanted our land and who took our fair-skinned children away to be civilised in a white man's world. Even now, there is limited tolerance and understanding of this country's first inhabitants. These attitudes have been felt and experienced by the majority of our peoples over many years. Though these attitudes have changed somewhat, Aboriginal people are still reeling from the years of racism, dispossession of our lands, denial of our languages and customs, incarceration into prisons and marginalisation to the fringes of the wider society, with little self governance of our lives, our families' wellbeing or of our culture and countries. This process of colonisation has deeply impacted on us and caused major problems for a large portion of our peoples collectively. So how do we go about creating a life that reflects our identity and the cultural expressions of our ancestors?

Over the last two decades my mother and Elders have passed on to me this cultural expression: our peoples practised our cultural beliefs and kinship obligations to our family groups, communities and country through a strict cultural and spiritual Aboriginal Law system. This consisted of special ceremonies between groups at significant times and places in country. Although we spoke different languages and came from various regions across Australia, our cultural knowledge, creation stories, songlines, dance ceremonies and the Law that governed us and all living things were similar in practice. We also had a strict code of ethics, respect for each other and for our and other peoples' lands. But carrying on the traditions of our ancestors, or even a small part of them, in contemporary times proves to be hard. So, how do we reclaim our heritage and self in the dysfunctional world that has now become our standard of life? How do we right things for ourselves and our children, as well as help those who are drowning in the despair that prevails nowadays?

As a Nyungar person, I have come to realise that to be able to understand the meaning behind my mother's words and the history of our collective peoples, the need to embrace culture and our knowledge is of the greatest importance. For me, it is fundamental in helping to heal the pain that I and many other Aboriginal people nationally have felt, from all those wrongs committed against us. The coming of others to our shores, claiming country as their own, introducing a new order – a way of thinking, speaking and acting – has negatively misplaced us, the First Peoples of our lands, in the scheme of things. This is one, if not the most fundamental, reason why we as a collective continue to display behaviours that are out of sync with who we are as Australians. The pain we felt from the changes to our lives in the past has also blinded us today, so that we disregard our spiritual and cultural inheritance that has been passed down through the generations. How do we go about bringing positive change to our lives, which would benefit us individually as well as enabling us to help empower our own families and peoples? Could a way be our own personal spiritual journeys? In healing ourselves, we then have a positive influence in our collective communities.

I share the journey I made, which also includes my family stories. This highlights the importance of valuing our own cultural and social knowledge and oral histories. What I have learned over time through my mother's voice – our stories are our history, and our history, our country – are fundamental lessons for us, as individuals and cultural communities. The responsibility is ours, as individuals and as a group, to reinforce this truth to our peoples and young ones as a positive goal, to reclaim our cultural ways.

MUMMY'S VOICE – HER STORIES, MY HISTORY

When asked, my mother always finds time to share information with me about everything Nyungar: the black side of my family's history. This shows me that the voices of our Old People can impart many important aspects of our cultural and social histories. These voices can also share the most amazing stories about our relations we might not have been aware of. These stories are so filled with rich information that libraries and the internet

Beryl Dixon, nee Keen, my mum, 2006 – a great believer in family and respect for our Elders. Courtesy Tjalaminu Mia

come a distant second in terms of knowledge. This is how my mother, as the senior Elder in my family, has become the best source of information for me on many fronts. Though she is nearing her 90th birthday, her memory is as sharp as a tack. She can recall the most detailed information about government policies, World Wars I and II, the changing landscape of country towns and Perth, various people, civic events and many other things; other people's knowledge pales in comparison. Most importantly, knowledge she can share about family members is a comfort and a great legacy. She can also remember the hard times her family and Nyungar people lived through. Her stories are full of oppressive conditions that were endured in silence by her family and other Nyungar peoples in the years of control and racism. She says this permeated across all our countries, affecting every Aboriginal person.

On a Sunday visit to see my mum, she cooked up her usual tucker, a roast dinner with all the trimmings. You could smell the delicious aroma well before you got to the front door. It was intoxicating, not because of hunger, but of what it represented. Sunday lunch at mum's has become a much valued ritual for more years than I can count. My brother, the poet, even wrote a poem about it. He speaks of family get-togethers that symbolise a united family, the shared laughter and the feelings of joy that come from a family coming together. These Sunday lunches have meaning for my siblings and me because of the years spent away from our mother and extended family when we were incarcerated in the Sister Kate's Children's Home. This home was established in 1933 and originally set up by Sister Kate to accommodate orphans and fatherless children sent to her from the Aborigines Department. With involvement of the Chief Protector of Aborigines, AO Neville, the purpose changed dramatically, and Aboriginal children were sent there on a 'skin colour' basis, enforcing the assimilation policies of the day. Living our early primary and adolescent years in the home caused us all to lose our sense of self and we didn't know where we fitted in the world anymore, especially with our mother and close family members.

These lunches now happen much less often due to my mother's age, yet I still make time to have a Sunday meal with her, to discuss family business and for her to share family stories with me. This is when I want to know more about our women Elders. The family photographs usually make an appearance, too, and the day becomes a walk down memory lane for my mum. With photos strewn all over the floor, making a tapestry of people's lives, I can see the delight and recognition in my mum's eyes of beloved family members. This proves to be a wonderful way of reconnection for her, to people she shared her life with. And for me, they provide a link – a connection to my Old People I would not necessarily have, as most of them passed away before I was born. I value these times because they disperse any feelings I might have at the time of 'aloneness'. When looking at photographs of family members while your mum's rattling off their names – who they are, their personalities, what they did and where they fit in the family – a picture starts to form in your mind of what these people were like. You start to know these ancestors a little better because you are becoming familiar with them as 'once real people' who played a role in your family and still have their spot on the family tree.

As my mum's stories unfold, I study the faces of the people in the photographs more closely. Those staring back start to seem very real. Though they have passed away, to me there still seems to be a sense of familiarity, a link between us. One could say I am romanticising elements of our culture, the spiritual connections we have with ancestors. I wonder sometimes whether I should stay silent or even lie to appease those who are sceptical of this form of cultural expression. But I cannot stay silent. There have been several occasions at my mother's house when I have felt a presence in the room with us, followed by a voice at whisper level calling my name. When this happens, I always look at my mum to see if she heard it too. But she acts like she hasn't noticed and I always end up asking, 'Did you hear that mum?' and her reply, 'No, it must be just for your ears.'

But she then says, 'Don't concern yourself, it's most probably the Oldies visiting too.' To me this signals that she did hear but was not going to make a fuss. I usually go back to looking at the photos but I can't help but notice at times that a calm energy descends over us and fills the room.

By the end of that particular Sunday, mum's house was electric from the happy energy, the laughter and love that came from the stories she shared about my relations. My mum is a spiritual person and has respect for people still living and those who have departed this world. She still refers to our older family members who have passed away as a part of her and our lives, and takes pride in being able to recall details about them and is open to sharing her stories.

GRANDMA FARMER – I HEAR YOUR WHISPER, CALLING

Seeking further connection to my Nyungar culture and family members led me to a major taproot of our family, Emily Farmer nee Coyne, my great-grandmother. I made a journey to seek her out as I felt she would ground me further in my identity. I also felt that knowing her better would help me to help my children and grandchildren. I did not want them to feel only half a person as I once did. I want them to feel whole, entire in who they are.

In my work as a research fellow in Oral History, Culture and the Arts in the School of Indigenous Studies at the University of Western Australia, my job was to provide vehicles for a collective Aboriginal voice through oral history publications. In these I was asked to share aspects of my life along with other Indigenous authors. In our last two books, *Speaking From the Heart* and *Heartsick for Country*, in my stories I introduced the reader to several people in my family, relations who have made significant contributions in helping me understand myself. Yet it is Emily who has been a constant in my thoughts, making her presence felt more and more. I felt and still feel a connection. Some time ago I embarked on a journey to find out more about her: what she was like, what she achieved in her life and what pathways she carved out for herself and her family, so she, her children and grandchildren could survive, in the days of oppressive white laws and control of our peoples, especially the stranglehold of the Native Welfare Department.

My mum often says, when sharing her memories about my great-granny,

> *Grandma Farmer was pretty savvy how things worked back then, and she was alert to what went on in the town we lived in while us kids were growing up. She made sure she got on with everyone and was always polite and charming, but no one could pull the wool over her eyes, she was one jump ahead.*

Emily Farmer, nee Coyne, with two of her daughters, Martha and Phoebe, Katanning, WA c. 1918. Courtesy Beryl Dixon

This made me want to delve further into who Grandma Farmer was because, listening to my mum, it seemed Emily was a feisty, strong black woman and I wanted to know her more. My journey took me down several roads: wading through Native Welfare files in various government departments, as well as other places that held notes of paper which made up, from the descriptions and interpretations of others, my great-granny's life. I also made trips to my country, walking in some of her footprints.

EMILY

Emily was born around 1857 and was taken from her mother at a very young age by the Aborigines Department to be placed with white people to be cared for, but also trained as a domestic servant. Getting to know her I found, as she grew to maturity, that Emily became a strong, capable Nyungar woman, who was devoted to the memory of her husband, William 'Peg' Farmer, born around 1863 and passing away in 1917. After his death, she never remarried and was the sole carer for her big family. She was also devoted to her children (15 in all, nine boys and six girls) and her grandchildren.

Both black and white people in the town where she lived held her in high regard. Her involvement in several community civic events, like the Anzac marches (four of her sons served in World War I, two dying on the battlefield), earned their respect. Another son served with the Second Australian Imperial Force in World War II and made it back home. A film titled *The Forgotten 2002* by Nyungar filmmaker Glen Stasiuk is based on Aboriginal servicemen and women who went to various wars to fight for their country but were overlooked in a multitude of areas on their return home. This film recognises their contributions and pays respect to their efforts and the sacrifices they made for their country. All four of my great-uncles are mentioned in this film. This makes me very proud and to add to my feelings of pride, Glen is my nephew and these ancestors are his great-great-uncles. I mention this because it highlights that there are younger generations in our family who are looking back to our Old People, wanting to know about family members, so they can walk into a more culturally grounded future. I hope my nephew continues to research his family history and help others in his role as a filmmaker to do the same. Emily also worked with Dr Campbell Pope, delivering babies and laying out deceased people in their homes.

What has very recently come to light is that my great-grandmother is noted for making a traditional Nyungar rug out of Bilby skins. This was some time in the 1920s. My mum has often mentioned to me that when she was a young girl, she remembers seeing and asking Grandma Farmer about some traditional cultural items she had – Dowitj, a killing stick for bush food, and Waardi, a fighting stick – that were kept out of sight from prying white eyes, under Emily's house. My mum and her sisters were not allowed to talk about these things to anyone outside the family home. I think this was one of my great-granny's strategies to keep some part of her culture alive, and the Aborigines Department away from her family and grandchildren.

I travelled to Katanning, a country town in the South West, where she made her home for near on 60 years, until her death in 1952. Strangely enough, her passing was not that long before I was born to one of her grandchildren, my mum Beryl, who she was very close to. This was because mum and several of her sisters stayed with Grandma Farmer to do their schooling while their parents worked in the bush clearing land for farmers from that region. Their relationship was so close that it has now spanned many years past the grave. My mother is the third-oldest grandchild and the oldest child of my great-granny's ninth child, daughter number two, Emily, her namesake. My mum's mother married Leonard George Keen in the mid-1920s and had my mum, their first child, Beryl, in 1926. Over the years my mum has shared quite a few of her experiences, which include many stories of her time spent with Grandma Farmer. Mum so loved her grandmother Emily and the love between them was reciprocal. Their connection was strong and didn't weaken as both got older, but rather became stronger as time passed. In fact, my mother was the one who, with her father Len and Emily's oldest son, great-uncle Harry, made all the necessary arrangements at the time of Emily's death. Her passing was a sad loss for family members, especially my mother. Of all the Old People she knew when growing up, the one she felt closest to was Grandma Farmer.

My mother has reached the close of her eighth decade, turning 90 on 19 November 2016. She is now the matriarch of six sets of family trees, made up of various relations in Nyungar families in the Great Southern region of southwest Western Australia: the Coyne, Farmer, Knapp, Keen-Hayward and Williams families of the Goreng and Minang peoples. I have a traditional name, but my mum was not given one, as was the case for her own mother. Though we were not aware of her having one, my great-granny could easily have had a traditional name that we did not know about. Her own mother had a traditional name: my great-great-grandmother Tuglaranu was a traditional Nyungar woman from the region around Albany, where Grandma Farmer was placed to work for a white couple by the name of Williams until she was in her late teens. Tuglaranu also had a European name – Suzannah Sivia. Being taken away from her mother when she was very young would have changed many things in Grandma Farmer's early years, even the use of a traditional name, if she had one. Her files state so and given that she had her daughter Emily with her in her early years, one would think that my great-grandmother would have also had a Nyungar name. We will never know this for sure.

Tuglaranu had several children – Native Welfare files show three: including my great-grandmother Emily, there was one boy named Ned or Fred and another girl named Louise, who the family called Lucy or Lizzy. My mother recalls knowing only Fred and Lizzy as her great-uncle and great-aunty. These Elder relations were born from a union between Tuglaranu and a Portuguese man named Tom Coyne. I am not exactly sure what he did to scratch out a living in our country or how they met, but he was in the region in the early part of the 1800s. He may have been a sealer, as Albany was one of the main supply bases for seal hunters in the southern ocean. These two people, the taproots of one of my family trees, the beginning of all the Coyne and Farmer descendants, have all but disappeared in the minds of our own younger family members who do not know their family history and in the archives of white bureaucracy. A sketchy trail gone cold, faded into obscurity. This obscurity has, in many ways, become the 'catch phrase' of lost identity of our people collectively.

There are no photographs of these ancestors in the government files I searched, just a few scraps of paper with scrawled notes handwritten by various people who made their appraisals from their own worldviews. They were either government officials or white anthropologists and would have been seen by our peoples as the aides of the white boordiya – bossmen of the government departments that made up white bureaucracy. In reality, they were really 'blind assessors': they didn't see the true picture, they only saw what they wanted to see. Their observations and interpretations would no doubt carry no thought of the hardship people endured in those days. It would have been a time of upheaval and change for both spouses, one being with a wadjela (whiteman) and the other frowned upon for taking up with a black woman, in a relationship that was doomed from the start really due to the government's control of white–black relations at that time.

The thoughts running through my head when I made my way to my mum's house on that Sunday were filled with the hope of her sharing further aspects of my great-grandmother Emily's life. My mum, sensing that I wanted to talk about family, was happy to share her memories and said,

'Nyungars had their backs hard against the wall in those early days, so we all stuck together like glue just to survive. Times were really hard for us then, and Grandma Farmer was the glue in our family. It's good that you want to know about your relations so you can pass the knowledge onto your girls and grannies.'

STRONG BLACK SISTERS

There are many reasons why I want to know Emily better and shadow her footprints, follow her down some of the roads she travelled. I want to explore the idea that some of the paths she carved out for herself and her family parallel the path of another family member, my aunty Joan Winch, who is a revered Nyungar Elder and advocate for Aboriginal health and human rights. As with Emily, she lost her mother when she was young and her first-born daughter passed away when she was in her forties, to the same kind of sickness as Emily's oldest girl, Myra, at the same age. Both these daughters passed away without giving their mothers grandchildren. Aunty Joan, like Emily, has had several tragedies in her life and has faced them, battled her way with an iron will and found strength from this to carry her through. She has also incorporated this strength into her professional life and this has inspired others of our people, especially our women, to do the same.

Like Emily, Aunty Joan has helped our women lighten the burdens from a sense of hopelessness and battle fatigue, which hamper their journeys. My aunty has faced her fair share of battles over the years and has survived, but in doing so still extended her hand to many others in their time of need. I feel Aunty Joan is the one who resembles Emily the most. Like Grandma Farmer, Aunty Joan is resilient, knows her own women's power, is happy in her black skin and has a strong sense of her Nyungar identity. She, like Emily, has carved out a road, a cultural pathway that constitutes the continuity of healing for her people as well as the reinforcing of her cultural identity. She has brought this about by placing herself in the areas of Aboriginal health education and cultural healing – similar strategies Emily used in her life. The difference is that Aunty Joan has added a national and international perspective in the contributions she has made to our peoples and the nation. Strangely enough, this respected Nyungar Elder, though close to my mother and aunties, did not play a significant role as one of my family Elders until later in my life. These last 25 years have brought for me cultural

Dr Joan Winch, nee Heath, my aunty – a great believer in spirit and a source of inspiration, 2006. Courtesy the author

realignment and a stronger sense of my own women's power and, with this, a pride in the contributions Aunty Joan has made in getting government agencies and Aboriginal people to recognise the need for better health care for our peoples and children. Over the years, aunty has also voiced her concerns regarding nurturing Aboriginal sisterhood and the importance for our women to acknowledge this. She would like to see more proactive action in this area by our women. I see my aunty as a respected Nyungar Elder in our collective communities and value her for the wonderful contributions she has made over the years to advance our collective peoples into a positive future.

REVISION – REAR-VIEW MIRROR, IS ME

My mum's words always warm my heart and make me feel stronger, knowing that my family members who have passed are still around in spirit to draw strength from. Listening to my mum talk about these individuals, I think this is a wonderful way to bridge gaps in family histories. Her stories also inspire me to want to seek out further information, to delve deeper into my family history so I will know people on a more intimate level, especially my old women ancestors. I would like to walk in their footprints, to make further journeys along some of the pathways they walked during their lives, deliberate pathways carved to combat oppression they faced in those times of major change. Oppression was a commonality for all our Old People, experienced one way or another. As I see it, an individual story is only that, but the collective story and experience – the common thread that runs through – makes up a tapestry of the struggles shared by them all. I also feel that by embarking on journeys, they can give us opportunities to reconnect to our ancestors. By doing this, we learn more about ourselves in the process.

I think our old ancestors still play an important role in our lives. Their presence, though a spiritual one, keeps us connected to the past. This is a wonderful legacy. We need to open our minds and hearts and embrace what is meant by 'the importance of reconnection'. Many of our peoples and younger generations may not see things this way and may not be aware of this potential. So, how do we go about changing things, so positive outcomes can happen? How do we, as a collective, present an opening that enables us to be more open ourselves, to the cultural and spiritual knowledge that our Old People wish to share with us?

One way that could be explored further is the value we place on family oral history. Our Old People's stories could help our younger generations feel closer to older family members. They could also be a way of confirming their identity as Aboriginal children. This should be a solid foundation to build bridges to reconnect our younger generations to their Aboriginal history, providing a cultural base to strengthen our young people's knowledge. Our Old People still have a vital role to play – as our family historians and storytellers. The stories about our ancient culture, through the voices of our Old People, are important. Our Elders could be seen as cultural teachers, in places designated as 'places of stories'. This could enable a 'rear-view mirror approach' to cultural grounding and for healing. This could be the catalyst that enables further cultural pathways to be carved out by our future generations, once they are 'knowledged up' and versed in the importance of cultural dialogue of our histories. The voice of the past – the old ways of our peoples – is being projected into the present, providing the foundations for new beginnings by our peoples.

We need cultural references that are based on practices and protocols which worked for millennia. These resulted in cultural solidarity and respect for others. From what I have personally experienced in my life, having to provide a base for cultural unification and respect for my children, grandchildren and now my first great-grandchild, after years living in children's homes, I see this as a positive way forward. We cannot expect our younger generations to move forward and into positions of positive leadership unless they appreciate themselves and their culture. They need to have opportunities that enable them to become culturally and spiritually grounded in who they are.

Some of the pathways that our children are walking now reinforce negative behaviours and are helping to manifest the present paradigm of further 'lost identity'. I feel very disconcerted to see this happening. This is why I feel passionate about the role our Elders and oral history can play in our own, and our young people's, lives. If we can see the importance of both, and the opportunities they can provide, our young ones may instead turn away from introduced ways and look towards our Elders for knowledge and guidance, and in the future once again walk our own cultural pathways.

CONCLUSION

My mother's words at the start of this chapter have helped vanquish the separation anxiety, the negativity and sense of hopelessness I once felt, resulting from being taken from my family in my younger years. Seeking out my great-grandmother has helped to bring further balance to my life and has grounded me in family and place. Seeking and finding Emily has been a celebration of my identity. She was a strong black woman who lived for 95 years and, in her long lifetime, was the strength behind her big family. I am very proud and feel blessed that Emily is the family taproot for me, my daughters, my grandchildren and my great-grandchild.

Having our Old People to refer back to is a powerful legacy, which we collectively should celebrate. Having a sense of who we are and place of belonging is what we pivot our lives around, but if you don't have this understanding, you can become lost. Before we can expect others to value us, we need to first see the value in ourselves. This comes from knowing who you are and where you come from. But this will always elude us if we don't acknowledge our Old People and the role they play in our lives, as well as their contributions to our wellbeing.

We need to learn the value of our cultural heritage. We need to nurture an awareness, understanding and pride of what it means to be First Peoples of country, whose inheritance of a spiritual and cultural knowledge base, which survived in all our peoples for thousands of years, remains even now the base of who we are. We need to once again secure this very knowledge within ourselves, our children and our communities. We can't achieve this outcome without a cultural strategy framework, introduced by us, for us, and delivered by our learned countrymen and women. It stands to reason, we need our Elders and their stories to make this work.

BIBLIOGRAPHY

Dixon, G (2003) *Holocaust Revisited – Killing Time*, School of Indigenous Studies, University of Western Australia, Nedlands.

Morgan, S and Mia, T (2002) *Echoes of the Past: Sister Kate's Home Revisited*, Centre for Indigenous History & the Arts, School of Indigenous Studies, University of Western Australia, Nedlands.

Morgan, S, Mia T and Kwaymullina, B (2007) *Speaking from the Heart*, Fremantle Arts Centre Press, Fremantle.

Morgan, S, Mia T and Kwaymullina, B (2008) *Heartsick for Country*, Fremantle Arts Centre Press, Fremantle.

Primary sources

Nyungar Artefacts & Cultural Material, File No. H99.475, Western Australian Museum, Perth, *c.* 1920s.

Western Australian Department of Native Affairs/ Welfare Files – No. 338 -30, Personal Card no. A. 966 on Emily Farmer, nee Coyne, Department of Aboriginal Affairs, Perth.

EMERITUS PROFESSOR MARYANN BIN-SALLIK

Ed.D (Harvard) is a member of the East Kimberley Djaru Nation; born in Broome and raised in Darwin from the age of nine. She was the first Indigenous Australian to work in the higher education sector and the first to obtain a Doctorate from Harvard University. In 1989, MaryAnn gave up a successful nursing career of 17 years to become an academic and structured her career towards improving access and equity for Indigenous Australians. MaryAnn retired as Dean of Indigenous Research and Education at Charles Darwin University in 2008 but continued to sit on university and government boards and committees. In 2016, she was headhunted by Western Sydney University and became Pro-Vice Chancellor Indigenous Leadership.

TRUTH AND CONSEQUENCE

MaryAnn Bin-Sallik

Never in my wildest dreams did I ever imagine that I could, or would, study at university. If, as a young child growing up in Broome, someone had said to me, 'MaryAnn, you are going to be the first Aborigine to graduate as a trained nurse from the Darwin Hospital', I would have looked at them blankly because from my worldview, at that time, it was only people from the wider Australian community who became nurses. As well as being too shy to respond, I would have been puzzled by this place called Darwin, as I had not heard of it.

Twenty-six years later in Darwin, the year before I gave up nursing in 1974, had someone asked me, 'Do you know that you will leave Darwin to live in Adelaide? That you will give up nursing and you will come back to Darwin in 2001 as a university professor and dean of a faculty based on Aboriginal cultures, heritage and histories?', I would have thought that they were out of their mind. Darwin did not have a university then, nor were there any Aboriginal professors in Australia, and the Aboriginal cultures, heritage and histories discipline did not exist.

So, I will be taking you on a journey starting from my early childhood to where I am now, from a standpoint of truth and consequence; that is, my truth, and the consequences of my truth that have shaped and moulded my life as a strong, proud Aboriginal woman. I know when to call upon my ancestors for guidance and when to beckon my spirit.

A GOOD LISTENER AND A KEEN OBSERVER

I was born into the Aboriginal community of Broome, in Western Australia's Kimberley region, on the land of the Yaru Nation on 2 November 1940, to an Aboriginal mother and a Malay pearl diver father. I identify as an Aborigine. I believe that I was born under a lucky star in spite of, or maybe because of, it being not only the Feast of All Souls in purgatory, according to my mother's Catholic religion, but also the year of the Golden Dragon, which comes once in every 60 years in the Chinese calender. Anyway, for whatever reason, I believe I was lucky because I was not removed from my family, unlike my mother and her mother before her and like many of my peers.

I was an only child until around the age of six when my brother Albert, aged five, appeared as a surprise one day. I was so excited and just loved him at first sight. He was my mother's orphaned first cousin. My parents took him in and raised him as their own to prevent him being placed in an institution. They could not adopt him, as dad was an alien. We were raised in a stable household surrounded by a large, loving extended family. Before Albert came to live with us I had regular sleepovers at the Catholic girls' orphanage for Aboriginal girls; those children were my cousins and friends. At that time I did not realise that they were part of the Stolen Generations from the Kimberley.

I have great memories of growing up in Broome, where my identity was forged. Mum ensured that Albert and I were grounded in our kinship structures, obligations and relationships. Though being born into and having lived through and been affected by Australia's pernicious policies of segregation and assimilation, like most young children I was not fully aware of them so could not understand their full implications. This was also an era when it was said that 'children should be seen and not heard', and when corporal punishment was the order of the day. My mother was never hesitant to exercise corporal punishment, which always ended with her asking, 'What! Haven't you learned your lesson yet?' This resulted in my brother and I being very obedient children.

I went on to be a good listener to adult conversations and a keen observer of my environment. I knew that many of my relatives could not travel from one place to another without formal permission from some 'white-man' in the Department of Native Affairs. I knew that we had to get permission to visit family in Beagle Bay Mission but could not stay overnight. I knew that some members of our community were given what was called 'citizenship' and had to carry around a piece of paper to say that they were free persons, which meant they could not be imprisoned by the police.

These government policies also influenced the employment opportunities afforded our adults. I would frequently overhear the adults of our community saying, 'Oh, so and so has got a very good job'. These good jobs were from the bottom of the barrel. They were working in the cattle industry, the pearling industry and labouring jobs within local government, driving trucks or working as manual labourers for the males, and for the females the jobs were cooking, taking in laundry or entering into domestic service. From my earliest memories I understood that we were different from the non-Indigenous community and that our lives were bound by restrictions and theirs were not. But I also knew that they did not have as much fun as we did. How did I know? That I don't know – I just knew. It was probably because I was happy. I had observed that some members of the wider community preferred to be with us and I had not observed any of the Aborigines wanting to be on the other side of the fence, so to speak.

Australia was the world leader in a deep-sea pearling industry that lasted from the 1850s to the mid-1950s and comprised three pearling ports: Broome in the Kimberley, Darwin in the Northern Territory and Thursday Island in Queensland. Hundreds of Asian men were brought to Australia to work in the pearling industry under the indentured labour scheme. This permitted them to work only within the industry, in one of the three pearling ports. If they went anywhere else in the country, they were deported back to their country of origin. These men came from China, Hong Kong, Indonesia, Malaya, Japan, Singapore and the Philippines.

Because of the pearling industry, Broome was a predominantly Asian town. Its official trade language was Malay, which was spoken by many Aboriginal men who worked in pearling. Many of the Asian men took Aboriginal brides, who also learned to speak Malay. My mother was a very fluent speaker of Malay. My brother and I were allowed to learn only some words, a few phrases and to count in Malay as it was my parents' secret language, so I missed out on a lot of information when the adults talked in Malay. Many of the Asian men integrated into the Aboriginal community and many of their cultural influences, words from their languages and features of their cooking are still evident today. Aboriginal identity in those former pearling towns, though based on classical Aboriginal cultures, was influenced by the classical Asian and classical European cultures, whereas in most other parts of Australia, the Asian influence is absent. Many Aboriginal descendants of Asian deep-sea pearlers, including myself, prefer to holiday in Asia where we have an understanding of the cultures and languages, where we can fit into the crowd and not be subjected to racism. We also go to Asia to visit our relatives and in turn they visit us.

Through my Asian connection I learned about the White Australia policy, to which my Asian father and maternal grandfather were subjected. I listened to adult conversations about Australia being scared of Asians, of 'The Yellow Peril' taking over our country and turning it into an Asian continent. Of course, at the same time, Australia's colonisers were trying to turn our black continent into a white one through the policies of segregation and then assimilation, and to rid Australia of what they perceived to be 'the black problem'. To us these policies were genocidal.

At first I did not realise that the segregation, assimilation and White Australia policies were also responsible for not allowing the Asian and Aboriginal communities to socialise with or participate in activities within the non-Indigenous community. I clearly remember my parents hosting regular dances in our home for members of the Aboriginal and Asian communities. It was not until much later, however, that I could make sense of the implications. As my knowledge base broadened, I learned that the Spanish had colonised the Philippines, my maternal grandfather's country of origin; that the British had colonised Singapore, my father's birthplace; that the Dutch had colonised Indonesia, the country of origin of my father's parents and older siblings; and that Australia had been colonised by 'Mother England'. From a fairly early age I had a child's understanding of how the 'white-man' (using the language of that era, which also meant the colonisers or the system of control) also colonised other Indigenous people to whom I was bound through affinal, consanguine and classificatory kinship ties. Importantly, many non-Indigenous (white) men and women had been integrated into our communities through marriage and were not viewed as the proverbial 'white-man' because they were our kin. So, early on I had a worldview that had horizons outside Australia, and the seeds of colonisation had already coloured my worldview. I believe this to be the reason why I am a big picture person and am global in my thinking, and why I am very much a humanitarian.

It was common to hear such things as, 'Oh, 'white-man' did this or that because he thinks he is smarter than us. But we know he is not smarter than us.' Mum was always saying that she was either smarter than or as smart as 'white-man'. It was one of her constant mantras. Consequently, I grew up knowing that the 'white-man' was not smarter than us.

I was also exposed to the various religions from Asia as well as Catholicism, because we were colonised by the Catholics. One day, when I was about five or six years of age, I asked my Muslim father to tell me about Mohammedanism, as it was called then. Dad very casually told me that there was only one God and that we all worshipped that same God in our different ways. Dad's response made absolute sense to me because the Catholic nuns had taught us there was only one God. The truth of the matter, however, was that dad was my hero – I hung on to and believed every word he uttered. So, from then on I have been open to all religions and have never questioned other people's religious beliefs.

I was not able to clearly understand or articulate everything I had heard or seen during my childhood in Broome, nor could I remember various things, probably because I did not place any great importance on them at the time. They were stored in my subconscious, however, and surfaced when I was mature enough to fully understand their messages and implications. I realise now that I learned to appreciate the differences in my community, within my extended family and, most importantly, within my immediate family. I believe it is this gift from my early life that has enabled me to enjoy cultural and religious diversity, making me a tolerant person with a strong sense of who I am.

THE CRUEL AWAKENING

In 1950 my family relocated to Darwin, the land of the Larrakia Nation, where my father had obtained work in the pearling industry. Our family's transition was relatively easy due to Darwin's proximity to the Kimberley region, where kinship ties had been forged from heroic times during the Dreaming. The other big plus was that the Aboriginal community in Darwin was very similar to that of Broome, due to the pearling industry and associated Asian influences and connections.

I was about 12 years old when the impact of the policies of segregation and assimilation became clear to me. For instance, in Broome I thought that the adults chose not to socialise with people from the wider community, but in Darwin I soon understood that they were not allowed to do so by law, that they could be prosecuted and even sent to prison. The Darwin Aboriginal community had its own social club, The Sunshine Club, and my parents were members. This club was also politically motivated and had an alliance with the Federal Council for the Advancement of Aborigines and Torres Strait Islanders, the body responsible for not only bringing about, but also ensuring the overwhelming success of, the 1967 Referendum that resulted in the federal government taking overall responsibility for Indigenous Australians, and Indigenous Australians being included in the Australian census. I discovered that the children I had befriended and played with from the Retta Dixon Aboriginal Children's Home, like the girls from the orphanage in Broome, were not orphans. They had been removed from their families and placed in religious institutions through government policies. I realised that my mother and grandmother had also been removed, for the same reason as these children: because they were 'mixed race' children. The things I had taken for granted in Broome all started to make sense as they were acted out in Darwin, especially as I now understood the impact and unfairness of it all. This was a profound experience for me, a cruel awakening that wiped out my childhood innocence.

My brother and I attended the local Catholic school and I finished primary school in 1954. The system in operation at that time was that non-Indigenous children were given the opportunity to sit exams for scholarships that enabled them to go interstate and obtain a better secondary education than was offered in Darwin. The Indigenous boys undertook exams to gain apprenticeships and the only option for Indigenous girls was domestic service. I was 14 years of age and, for the past couple of years, had been visualising myself as a nurse in a crisp blue uniform. I got the message loud and clear that 'white-man' had determined that, as a black female, I was not even entitled to the option our males were given. I thought, 'What happened to mum's mantra that "we are as clever as white-man?"' I announced to mum that I was not going to be a domestic and she casually said, 'No, that's right MaryAnn. You are going to boarding school and you will become a secretary.' That was her dream for me as she saw secretarial work as one of those new 'good jobs' to which I should aspire. I just looked at her, dumbstruck. I knew better than to contradict mum, and I also knew that I was safe and was not going anywhere because my parents did not have the money to send me anywhere. This was well before the availability of Commonwealth scholarships to boarding school for Indigenous youth. My mother was determined that her children were going to have the opportunities she had never had, and she wasn't afraid of the hard work or risk-taking that might be required in capitalising on those opportunities. In time, thanks to my mother, I became a very determined and ambitious person, always ready to create or capitalise on opportunities, not afraid of taking risks. I believe that what stops us most in life is our fear.

In Broome, mum had been a small-business woman. She owned and managed a milk bar and managed the family's small fish business while dad was at sea. In Darwin, at the time mum was contemplating sending me to boarding school, we were living at a place called Winnellie, which was in the sticks. It was a long way out of town with no corner store and a very poor bus service. Within no time mum had turned a part of our house into a corner store and our family car into a taxi. She was the first Aboriginal woman owner-taxi driver in Darwin. By this time dad was no longer diving. He was driving trucks and he would come home from work and drive the taxi. He also ran illegal gambling games. This gave my parents the means to send me to boarding school in Adelaide in 1955, and my brother the following year. I spent three years at boarding school and my parents could afford to only bring me home for Christmas breaks. By insulating me from the realities of my life, boarding school gave me the space and confidence to determine the choices that I wanted in life. On returning home to Darwin at the end of boarding school, I had already made up my mind that no-one was ever going to tell me what to do with my life. Not 'white-man' or even my own mother. I was determined to be my own person.

CAREER CHOICES

I commenced my four-year nursing training in February 1958 and became the first Aboriginal student nurse at the Darwin Hospital. And was I in for a big shock, for I was about to learn of and experience racism at all levels. On a personal level, I was the only nurse there who ever had to do all early morning shifts, 6.00am to 3.30pm, for six months straight. In my first two years of nursing I was mostly rotated between what were called the native wards, which catered only to traditional Aboriginal people, and the children's wards. I had a couple of very short stints in the wards for the wider community and the Aboriginal people who were to be assimilated. I found the medical staff and student nurses were great to work with, but a lot of the trained nurses, or sisters as they were called back then, were overtly racist towards me and were forever giving me bad reports, as did a small number of patients who protested that my nursing procedures were substandard. I was lucky, however, because some senior nursing staff knew that I was a hard worker and was eager to learn. They soon realised that the negative reports against me were always from the same few staff members so they set in place procedures to curtail the negativity against me.

Nursing was where I witnessed the full impact of the official policies of assimilation and segregation, and I learned all about institutional racism and genocide while working in the native wards. For instance, after delivering their babies, Aboriginal women were often sterilised without their permission. Very few of these women could speak English and therefore they did not understand what was happening to them. I witnessed that in most instances when Aboriginal children died in the middle of the night, the doctors would not get out of bed to examine them and certify their death. The children would be placed in grey army blankets and left on the cement floor in a corner of the ward until the doctor came on duty at 8.00am.

Despite all the negativity and racism I enjoyed nursing, especially among my own people, where I felt safe. Furthermore, most of the domestics, gardeners and grounds people working at the hospital were Aborigines or Torres Strait Islanders, who also gave me a lot of support. There were times when the racism got the better of me and I wanted to leave nursing but thanks to the love, support and encouragement I got from my own people, I knew I needed to stay the distance. They would tell me over and over again that I had to stay and become our first trained nurse. This is what being Aboriginal means to me. This is when I learned how much love there is in our community.

Nursing was the making of me. Though I had the support of my family and community, I had to walk every step of the way by myself in the regimented and hierarchical world of nursing, making decisions for myself. Through it all I was able to discipline myself to stay focused on my goal. To do this I celebrated the small victories and milestones along the way. Despite the morbid nature of the work, I trained myself to only dwell on the positive aspects of my life. I was able to achieve despite racism. I graduated from nursing in February 1962, becoming the first Aborigine to graduate from the Darwin Hospital. My first nursing appointment was at Hooker Creek Aboriginal Reserve in the desert country of the Northern Territory. I spent 13 years working as a trained nurse, mainly in Darwin Hospital's casualty unit. I had two stints on cattle stations and my final nursing job was with a neurosurgeon.

In 1974 I left Darwin with my two daughters, aged 11 and nine years, to make a new life in Adelaide on the land of the Kaurna people. I was expecting to get a nursing position real quick but I could not break through the racial barriers in Adelaide at that time. I spent nine months on the supporting mother's pension and most of that time I was seeking employment. My children and I shared a dilapidated house with a friend and her two children, and sat on the floor to have our meals.

This all became too much for me. I knew that I would have to give up nursing, but only temporarily, until my girls and I got on our feet. In February 1975 I commenced work at the South Australian Institute of Technology, now the University of South Australia, as the student counsellor to its Aboriginal Task Force (ATF) program, which was the first Indigenous higher education program in Australia. I became the first of our people to work within the higher education sector in Australia. I worked full-time, studied social work part-time and raised my children full-time on my own. For the first time ever, Aborigines were afforded the opportunity to study within the hallowed halls of academia. I was so inspired by the students who came from all over the country, so energised with hope and aspiration. Within no time I knew that I would never return to nursing and that I had found a new passion and a new career.

The ATF provided the blueprint for the Indigenous higher education sector. Every university in Australia now has an Indigenous program and there are some 10,000 of our people studying at universities. There are now many Indigenous academics at the level of associate professor, professor, dean, pro vice-chancellor and deputy vice-chancellor. It is important to note that there are more Indigenous females than males working in the sector, more females in the student population, and more female graduates and postgraduates than male. No-one has attempted to fully research this phenomenon to date.

CONCLUSION

My life has been a bountiful tapestry of Aboriginal experiences and lessons in learning. I have always worked as a professional and made my own career choices because many people believed in me. My mother taught me to believe in myself. She showed me, by her own actions, the importance of taking risks to achieve one's goals and how to create and capitalise on opportunities. The Aboriginal community in Broome gave me my earliest memories of community love and nurturing, and my Asian connection provided me with a wider view of the world, one that introduced me to Indigenous peoples of Asia to whom I am connected, and in later years gave me the knowledge to expand my horizons and to think globally. The Aboriginal community of Darwin gave the support I needed to complete my nursing training and the Nunga community in Adelaide gave me a job and supported me for the 27 years that I lived on their country. The love and support I have received from Aboriginal people throughout my life has given me the strength to achieve my dreams and aspirations. This is my truth and the consequences of my truth that have shaped my life, giving me the strength to push boundaries, make the most of opportunities and advocate along with my Indigenous brothers and sisters for a better Australia for us, the original inhabitants, of this Black Continent.

PROFESSOR JOAN WINCH (Heath) was born in Perth, Western Australia, on 9 June 1935. Her Mother was taken from Martu country (central Western Australia) in 1906 and her father's family was from Menang country (Nyungar). Professor Winch is a well-known leader and Elder and has worked tirelessly for Aboriginal people since the 1970s. In 1977 she gained a Bachelor of Applied Science in Nursing at the Western Australian Institute of Technology (now Curtin University). She went on to study midwifery and childcare. In 1983 she founded the Aboriginal Health Workers Program, Marr Mooditj college, in Perth, integrating a traditional Aboriginal approach to health and healing with Western medicine. In 1987 she studied ophthalmology under Fred Hollows though the University of New South Wales. In 1994 she gained a Masters in Public Health and Tropical Medicine at James Cook University. Joan's awards include WA Citizen of the Year (1987), Western Australian Aboriginal of the Year (1987), Australian Aboriginal of the Year (1987), the World Health Organization Sasakawa Award for Primary Health Care Work (1987) and Curtin University's John Curtin Medal for her services to the community. Joan was awarded her PhD in Aboriginal Studies from the Centre for Aboriginal Studies, Curtin University, in May 2011, four weeks prior to turning 76.

ABORIGINAL WOMEN AND LEADERSHIP: UP CLOSE AND PERSONAL

Joan Winch

I come from two Aboriginal bloodlines: Martu/Wongi people, whose country is inland southwestern Australia, and Nyungar, the coastal people of the South West. My mother was born in Martu Country, in Wiluna, in 1904. She was taken from her family in 1906 and sent to the coast. Because she was so young when she was removed she was not able to tell us anything about her background, such as her family name, who her relations were or anything about her culture, language or skin group. These points are very important for Aboriginal people to state on introduction to other people – you need to be able to say what family and group you are from and where your people are from. My mother lived and died without knowing about these connections. I started to seek out this information 30 years later.

In Wiluna, Martu Country, the local Aboriginal people heard via the 'bush telegraph' that I was looking for information about my mother and in 1981, 33 years after my mother passed away, I had a message from the Martu people to come to Wiluna on the pretext that they wanted some health advice. With other members of the health team from the Aboriginal Medical Service in Perth, I arrived there on Melbourne Cup day. On arrival, I was asked to come by myself to the special ceremonial grounds in the morning.

When I went, there was a big circle of people gathered. I was led to a place to sit down on the ground and about half a dozen men proceeded to shout and throw spears, yelling and shouting in language. I must have looked frightened because a young man next to me said, 'Don't be frightened. They are telling you the story of the 'one that was taken' as you are the daughter.' I was overwhelmed with emotion. I hadn't felt that there was anything missing in my life, but all of a sudden I felt that a giant jigsaw puzzle had just come together inside me. They had kept the story in their songlines dating back from 1906. I always used to think that had my mother known her roots, she may not have died at the young age of 44 years.

My mother was brought up in various church missions: Dulhi Gunyah at Victoria Park, Carrolup (now Marribank) at Katanning and Moore River Settlement, north of Perth. The mission girls were only taught the basics they needed to know about how to write a grocery list, read a cookery book, clean a house. I expect they had plenty of experience minding children at the mission, when the little children were incarcerated.

Missions and reserves were like concentration camps. Inmates were treated like prisoners and severely reprimanded if they absconded from the mission. For instance, there was a tin shed at Moore River called 'the boob'; people were incarcerated for any misdemeanour, real or imagined by their 'caretakers'.

When my mother was taken from the Wongawol family, she was renamed Lena Bookett, and her first job at 14 years of age was at the Ortons' farm called 'Petworth Park' at Moora. At the farm, with more Western food available, she was told that she was putting on too much weight to be called Lena so she was renamed Lily. Mum made a joke of it and said she couldn't be called Lena because she was too fat, but it was worse when she had to bring out the food for visitors to the dining tables and out came a 'black Lily' to serve the dinner guests; however, the name remained Lily until her death.

My mother was deeply controlled under the Native Welfare Act 1905, so every action was accountable to that system. The 1905 Act legalised the removal of Aboriginal children from their natural families, encouraged establishment of reserves and missions and introduced many restrictive measures over these Aboriginal people.

My father was more fortunate and had a luckier introduction to life. His mother was a Nyungar and Portuguese mixture – a legacy from the Portuguese sealers in the Bremer Bay area – and had the surname of Coyne. His father was a stonemason brought out from Cornwall in England to help build houses in the colony; many of these solidly built houses are still in evidence today at Katanning. My father, who was born in 1900, was not under the regulations of the Native Welfare Department, which enabled him to grow up as a free thinker and to have a freer childhood than my mother. He was able to make decisions about where he worked, was not subject to curfews, could sit where he chose in movie theatres, could go into hotels and could choose who he wanted to marry without requiring permission. Even so, the 1905 Act, which gave the Chief Protector full control of all natives, was ever present in all Aboriginal peoples' lives in Western Australia, dictating all aspects of living.

When I was two years old in 1937, in the middle of the great depression, my father moved our family to Fremantle. He saw Fremantle as having more opportunities for his children. He said that many Aboriginal children were excluded from school in the South West and he wanted us to have a good schooling.

We were the only Aboriginal family in the district so we didn't see ourselves as any different than the rest of the school kids. The 1905 Act was not significant to me then as I didn't know about having to be off the street by 6pm or alcohol restrictions for Aboriginal people. I did have some understanding about Aboriginal people not being welcomed into accommodation in hostels and hotels, as mum used to send my older brother and me down to the wharf when a troop ship came in so that we could invite returning Aboriginal soldiers back home. We had to crawl through large coils of barbed wire, which blocked off the wharf, and then clamber over the slippery barnacled rocks to get onto the wharf and wait by the gangway for our Aboriginal soldiers to disembark. We would shout out loud, 'Mum says come home!' I don't know how my mother knew about the comings and goings of troop ships as shipping movements were supposed to be a military secret. It must have been heart-rending for those brave men to have fought in a war zone only to be totally disregarded on their return to their own land. Some found on many occasions that their children had been taken away and put in missions. There were no War Service Homes for most of these Aboriginal returned servicemen and their pay packets were considerably less than the other soldiers. In their homeland they were redundant and marginalised in society.

NURSING

My mother died in 1948 when I was 13 years old. Soon afterwards, I started my career in nursing. I worked in many hospitals and travelled from Perth to Queensland. I often landed myself in a lot of bother as I was taught to stick up for the 'underdog'. However, I didn't realise that people did not want an Aboriginal person in their corner and I was beginning to understand that there were different rules for Aboriginal people, especially in Western Australia and Queensland. Things were much more difficult for me than for others. When I complained about workplace issues, a lot of 'my colleagues' wiped the floor with me and were willing to point the finger at me, indicating that 'I' was the troublemaker. Looking back over the years I see that there was much racism and sexism in my life. For instance, in 1955 I decided to return to Western Australia and take up psychiatric nursing at Heathcote Hospital. I loved the study and spent a good deal of time with books in off-duty hours. I came to grief with the establishment, however, and was sent packing after a confrontation with the night matron. She came to inspect the nurses' quarters and check if all the nurses were in bed. I was up and had had a few drinks at the hotel previously; as hotels shut at 9pm at that time, it was a couple of hours since I'd had a drink so I felt I was quite sober and behaving well. I was getting my clothes ready for work the next morning. I used to be very particular about having shiny shoes (a soldier I knew who had very shiny shoes told me the secret was to put methylated spirits in the shoe polish). The bottle of spirits had spilt and there was a suggestion that I was drinking methylated spirits in my room! I had to face the hospital board the next day. Though it was not spelled out that they suspected I was drinking methylated spirits, the implication was still there. I was asked to leave. I was heartbroken because I loved the work very much. I felt vindicated later in life when I surpassed the rest of the nurses who were in that group in terms of professional progress.

Having said this, one of my earliest experiences of successful struggles against inequality or unfair treatment was in the hospital system. When I was 18 years old, I was working at a Queensland psychiatric hospital. There was a strict hierarchical system in place based on seniority. I had gained some time and seniority and they put a junior nurse in charge of the shift instead of me, as it should have been. I was much more experienced and senior but she was put in charge. I was shocked and offended. I approached the Australian Workers Union. They supported me and instigated a rolling strike. All the nurses went out on strike and even though the hospital brought in other nurses from the capital, they eventually agreed with the union and reinstated me in the position that I should have been in from the beginning. The hospital valued me and later, when I left, they tried to get me to stay, refusing my resignation.

In 1980, after I gained triple certificate rating in General, Midwifery and Child Health nursing, I was engaged to work as the only community nurse attached to the Aboriginal Medical Service (AMS) catering for Aboriginal people in the Perth and metropolitan area. I was appalled when I realised the Aboriginal people in and around Perth were in a time warp. The ill-health problems I suffered as a child were still running rife in the community 40 years later: impetigo, scabies and head lice, together with gastro-intestinal tract and respiratory tract diseases complicated by lack of adequate housing. There were many Aboriginal people living in tents, car bodies, under bridges and in paddocks in and around Perth and the colourful names of these were very descriptive – 'Millers Cave' (car bodies), named after the Charlie Pride hit tune, 'Bull Paddock' and even 'The Bronx'.

This situation galvanised me to develop an Aboriginal health workers training course, which would educate Aboriginal people to provide health-care help and education to our own people. When I first suggested this at the AMS, the white doctor there was sceptical and extremely scathing that I could even think I could develop and implement this idea. He said with disbelief, 'You! Are you going to set this course up?' Despite this scepticism and considerable sabotaging, I persevered and this was how the Good Hands College – Marr Mooditj Health Worker Training Program was started 25 years ago. It remains one of the leading community-controlled Indigenous health training courses in the country. I was the founding director here for 20 years and remain on the board. Although this has been my main commitment, I have taken up many other roles during my professional career, particularly in leadership.

RACISM AND SEXISM

Back in my younger days, for Aboriginal women it was hard to have your say. That white male doctor who was so scathing about my ideas and potential was only one of many. While I shared my vision with and had the support of many Aboriginal leaders in the community, there were many Aboriginal men in the organisation who also opposed the idea and sabotaged the development in every way they could. One of my white female colleagues also joined in opposition. The idea of the course was very radical back then. It was a culturally appropriate course that challenged the mainstream dominant medical paradigm and power. Those in opposition accused us of teaching students to cheat because part of the learning was group classes and care of each other. We were trying to move away from individualised competitive learning to group empowerment pedagogy. Around that time in the 1970s I was one of the most highly qualified Aboriginal nurses in the country, but it seemed that Aboriginal sportsmen were much more valued in management roles. They seemed to be more desirable and were selected before me on various management positions and boards. The international forums were much more welcoming – less sexist and racist – and I was invited to many countries after developing the course.

Going overseas was an amazing experience for me. For the first time I was free from the relentless racism that pervades every aspect of your life and all your interactions. I felt as if a huge mantle of oppression had been lifted off me – and I had not even realised it was there in the first place. I felt released from bondage. I really wanted to take every Aboriginal person overseas so that they could experience this freedom. When we were out of the country, we were taken for who we were, just as people, as human beings; there was not a deep-seated unconscious historical relationship between white and black Australians, the colonised and the coloniser. This dynamic was absent and in that absence there was an enormous insight to how we were caught in it.

When I encounter racism, I try to confront it immediately in a firm but non-aggressive manner. Then it never burns me up. I don't go home angry and wondering if it really happened. Our society is still a racist society but some of us Aboriginal people are oblivious to this and we have become accustomed to it. If we allow ourselves to be held in bondage and oppression, so we will become bound and oppressed.

Recently I was asked whether things had become better or worse for Indigenous people in the last 50 years. I think that things have become much better in many ways but much worse in other ways. We had much more racism, less respect, fewer opportunities, too few of us taking up leadership and far less positive presence in the media in the old days. But nowadays we still have high rates of imprisonment, domestic violence and child abuse (and just because these were not disclosed does not mean they were not happening back then). Today, still, we have racism. We didn't have native title, the range of community organisations and programs, and some of the magnificent gains we have made. Yet, some things do seem worse nowadays. Our terrible statistics on health, suicide, employment, education and in the justice system have more or less stayed the same, and some have become worse. There is a sense of frustration. As some problems were beginning to be sorted, other new problems have emerged requiring different focuses and different skills and qualities from us.

Racism might have become less prevalent but the Pauline Hanson years signalled a resurgence of racism. During the times when she first got into parliament (in the 1990s), I was actually afraid for my safety. I remember once around that time I was in my car in a queue and the car behind me had some loud youths yelling out racist comments. It was frightening. I think that the police still continue racism. I have been abused by police and the justice system in my interactions with them over the years. While some huge advances have been made in some areas, I think that Aboriginal organisations are still made to be more accountable to the funders and that funding requirements are done at such minute detail than possibly is not imposed on non-Aboriginal organisations. This is a form of institutionalised racism. The dismantling of our elected body, the Aboriginal and Torres Strait Islander Commission, is a form of racism. ATSIC had problems but we wanted those to be fixed, not to abolish the whole structure. Now we do not have a representative body.

Racism is worse for Aboriginal women as there still is a perception that a man can do things better. We have had to work harder and better than anyone else, even now, to be accepted. I have seen this in the organisations that are controlled by men; they get funding more easily, they are treated more as equals and colleagues, and they seem not to need the same qualifications that we do, while women are devalued, paid less and treated with suspicion. Aboriginal women have been and still are very active in the workforce. The media has played a strong role in reinforcing racism and sexism. They seek out male Aboriginal leaders as spokespeople.

Aboriginal women appear to be undertaking more education than men. At Marr Mooditj, there were ratios of about 15 women to two men. However, when we had visitors, especially international ones, the women would look to the men time and time again to be the spokespeople, even though the men did not know as much as the women. Women still give up their power to the men. I was brought up in a culture where men had the power: for instance, men in households had all the say, so we have been socialised into not being equal, we have to learn to speak up. I expect that younger Aboriginal women will be more assertive given that they have grown up in a different social environment. I believe that our colonial history is responsible for this sexism. When colonisation occurred the men were conquered and the women enslaved and used as sexual slaves. The oppressed will oppress others and so men have oppressed the women – it is a cycle of oppression. Many women in the old days would have accepted that oppression, they had no choice. Male oppression might be imprinted on us so we tend not to assert ourselves or challenge the men when necessary. Women were taught to be submissive. If you get put down and you assert yourself, you are seen as unnatural and taking over a male role, so you forfeit your femininity. This goes for both Aboriginal and non-Aboriginal groups. It is important to teach women to be appropriately assertive and men to listen.

RAVE ABOUT US

My daughter and I developed an acronym for an Aboriginal women's leadership workshop we undertook in 1999. We called it Rave About Us.

Role of the women has always been the nurturers in our society. This makes us the carers and the teachers by example in the home.

Always be reliable. Be there and don't keep changing your mind. Hang in there when the going gets tough – this is when the tough get going.

Vision must be clear. Share it with others. Get as many people interested in your vision as you can – friends, family and funding bodies.

Education must always play an important part in planning. For our children to succeed in the future, the name of the game is 'the paper chase'.

Avoid mysteries. It refers to plain, simple speech and understandings. Never present something as a hard task, make it look easy.

Be honest and credible. When you are in the public arena and you handle the truth badly, you can lose your credibility and people remember.

Observe detail. Care about what you are doing. Don't look over the other paddock and think that it's greener. Make yours greener instead.
Understand others. Develop listening skills; listen to knockers as well because there may be merit in what they say. Have a belief in yourself to carry out the job.
Tell others about your plans. Understand what you are doing and prepare others to take over and carry the force through. Too many good ideas have stopped dead when the developer leaves.
Undefeated in victory! Be brave and courageous in your trailblazing. Admit your mistakes and learn from them and then move on.
Soar like an eagle. Be able to fly high and to take in the big picture as well as focus in on detail.

The Aboriginal women participants loved this workshop; they felt empowered and supported.

CONCLUSION

Over my long career and community work I have seen and experienced considerable racism and sexism. Times have changed and, as mentioned, some things are for the better and some things have become worse.

I think that the answer to addressing sexism, to breaking the chains, in our communities is to empower both Aboriginal women and men. More men should be encouraged into education. This will empower them. Equality between the genders has to be the most important issue. In the community and across all different forums respectful conversations need to take place between Aboriginal men and women, where the men should listen to women and the women should identify the disempowering and sexist behaviours and attitudes that oppress them.

I have thought about leadership roles in my organisational and community experience, and I would advise Aboriginal women in any leadership position to remember that we are all social change agents. We are active parts of the struggle for social justice. The morals and ethics a leader has are important. I learned from my experiences that you should always be honest, non-judgemental and to value people, show that you think they are worthwhile. If you give your word on something, you need to keep it. As Aboriginal leaders, we need to remember our cultural background – we come from a culture that values inclusive and participatory ways of doing things. We might need to code switch sometimes to be effective in Western systems, but from an Aboriginal point of view there has to be group involvement in some issues.

PROFESSOR JEANNIE HERBERT was born in Derby and grew up in Broome. Her grandmother was a Nyikina woman from the Kimberley. Jeannie graduated as a primary teacher in 1963 and continues to work in education. Her experience spans all levels from teacher, school principal, guidance officer, program coordinator to Indigenous education consultant. Having graduated with a PhD from RMIT University in 2003, she was awarded the 2016 RMIT University Outstanding Alumnus Award Australia. In 2012, she was made a Member in the General Division of the Order of Australia (AM) for 'service to tertiary education, particularly through improvements to educational outcomes for Indigenous people, and to the delivery of learning opportunities across regional and remote northern Australia'. She is Foundation Chair of Indigenous Studies and the first Pro-Vice Chancellor – Indigenous Education at Charles Sturt University.

'WILL THE REAL ME PLEASE STAND UP?'

Jeannie Herbert

To understand how I, as an Aboriginal woman, acquired the intellectual traditions that have influenced my life, I must revisit the past – the memories of my life, my upbringing – to gain insights into how I became who I am. Using inference as my process of reasoning, I will identify those experiences that I consider have been central in shaping me as a person, a process of 'I am what I am, having become what I thought' aligning with Spinoza's suggestion that 'Self and mind are essentially one and the same' (cited in Basso 1996, p. 85).

In seeking to understand who I am, I need to consider critical issues of identity – who am I? – and representation – what do I stand for? This is not as easy as it may appear. In its simplest form, it has a physical connotation. I could stand in front of a mirror and draw inferences around what others see when they look at me. Physical appearance suggests a mother, grandmother, aunty and so on; my dress and grooming might imply a senior professional or manager. Interestingly, it is my physical image that often inspires non-Indigenous people to question my identifying as an Aboriginal person with the inference obviously based upon my skin colour. Being a fair-skinned Aboriginal person, I find such questions both insulting and sad for they clearly indicate that many Australians have yet to relinquish the colonial attitudes of the past. Perhaps this is not surprising given that colonial policies were instrumental in embedding such thinking in the national psyche, as the historical record reveals. For example, in 1924, my mother and her sisters, despite their very young ages, were taken from their family in Derby to be raised in an institution in Perth. This was during that period (1915–1936) when AO Neville was Western Australia's Chief Protector of Aborigines (Haebich and Reece 1988) and developing his model of biological absorption as a means of getting rid of Aboriginal people:

> *The key issue to Neville was skin colour. Once 'half-castes' were sufficiently white in colour they would become like white people. After two or three generations the process of acceptance in the non-Indigenous community would be complete, the older generations would have died and the settlements could be closed.* (HREOC 1997, p. 108)

Critically, perceptions of the reality underpinning contemporary Australian society are strongly connected to the capacity of non-Indigenous Australians to recognise and accept how the persistent impact of this nation's colonial history may have influenced their personal worldviews. Such acceptance is a vital first step in enabling individuals to take responsibility for fixing what has long been broken in this society.

I would argue that this failure to take responsibility for the past has critically elevated the importance of the visual aspects of identity. My mother and her sisters, having been told they were in the home because their mother didn't want them, spent much of their childhood separated from one another on the basis of their different ages, in an environment that focused on 'getting rid' of Aboriginal people and their 'different' cultural identity. My mother, a quiet, introverted woman, was a stern taskmaster who rarely spoke of her childhood. As the oldest of eight children, I was, from a very early age, given a high level of responsibility in running the house and rearing my younger brothers and sisters. Life was a serious business with little time for 'fun'. In retrospect, I realised that my mother's child-raising skills likely reflected her own upbringing. And, in reflecting on the long-term impact that institutionalisation may have had on her, I came to appreciate what it did to people, how it stripped individuals of any sense of self-worth. Such reflection ultimately enabled me to understand the intergenerational impact of my mother's upbringing on myself and my siblings. As I matured and grew professionally, I gradually developed the capacity for taking pride in myself and who I was. I learned to move beyond the personal, to understand that people who have no capacity for valuing difference are unlikely to value Aboriginal knowledges and epistemologies or appreciate the centrality of family influence within Indigenous societies. Such standpoints make it easier to ignore history and overlook the enormous diversity that is a characteristic of Aboriginal society, a consequence of traditional societal structures and the impact of the colonisation process. I believe my life history has influenced the inner self, the 'thinking' me.

Given that much of my personal life experience revolves around my long-term commitment to, and continuing work in, education, it is important that I acknowledge its enduring influence and considerable contribution in making me who I am today. My initial goal had been to gain the qualifications I would need to become a primary school teacher and get a job. Times change, however, and it became increasingly necessary for teachers to upgrade qualifications in order to ensure job security. Over time, my continuing engagement in external studies increased my motivation and, as the learning itself became the critical impetus, my educational achievements increased and I began to pursue different career pathways. Similarly, my growing engagement in research as a critical component of postgraduate studies enabled me to develop deeper insights and build new strengths, within both professional and personal contexts. I graduated with a PhD in 2003. This personal education journey allowed me to empower myself while discovering someone I had not realised existed. The result of my journey could be seen as reflecting Smith's arguments in favour of decolonising methodologies, in particular her assertion that,

> *Self-determination in a research agenda becomes something more than a political goal. It becomes a goal of social justice which is expressed through and across a wide range of psychological, social, cultural and economic terrains. It necessarily involves the processes of transformation, of decolonization, of healing and of mobilization of peoples.* (Smith 2001, p. 116)

There were many times when the journey was such a struggle I just wanted to give up but, having achieved the previously unimagined, I persisted in what I now realise was my 'life-changing' journey. My mother had instilled in me a deep and abiding belief in the value of education but I don't think even she could have envisaged where that belief would lead me. From her perspective, education could provide her children with the means of escape from the oppression that had marked her life. From my perspective today, education is the key that enables the individual to become whatever they want to be, whoever they want to be. Making decisions about one's personal identity becomes a matter of personal choice, not something decided by others. Developing the strength to make such choices is worthy of considerable personal pride.

In this chapter, I link my life experiences with my research findings in an attempt to identify the intellectual traditions that have shaped me. I will consider a range of factors that I call shaping influences, those experiences that have made me who I think I am. I seek to be deliberately provocative in questioning my own capacity to know who I am for the older I become, the more complex the answer to that question seems to be. While I suspect such reality is the result of my personal longevity, I would argue that it is equally reflective of the rich and varied experiences I have enjoyed in both my personal and professional lives. Having chosen to reflect on who I am within the context of the present, I will begin at the end, so to speak. I am Professor Jeannie Herbert AM, Pro-Vice Chancellor – Indigenous Education and Foundation Chair of Indigenous Studies at Charles Sturt University, a multi-campus, regional university located in New South Wales. While the university's main regional campuses are located in Wiradjuri country, enrolments also include Aboriginal and Torres Strait Islander students from across the nation; hence, it is critical that, within my role, I am able to effectively engage with the diversity of this student body and their respective communities. I know that my own life journey enhances my capacity to do this.

My career in education began in Western Australia with my 1963 appointment as a primary school teacher. Having taught across all levels of education from early childhood to university, I moved into the university sector in 1996 and have since gained a diversity of experience in various positions, including Director of the Oorala Aboriginal Centre at University of New England in NSW (1996–97); Director of the Centre for Aboriginal and Torres Strait Islander Participation, Research and Development at James Cook University (JCU) (1997); Head of the School of Indigenous Australian Studies at JCU (1998–2002); Chair of Indigenous Australian Studies at JCU in North Queensland (2001–06); and Director, then Vice-Chancellor, of the Batchelor Institute of Indigenous Tertiary Education in the Northern

Territory (2006–09). I am proud to have won a number of prestigious awards in the past decade but those that I consider most reflect the shaping values of my personal educational journey are: being awarded a Member in the General Division of the Order of Australia in 2012 for my service to tertiary education, especially improvements to educational outcomes for Indigenous people, and delivery of learning opportunities across regional and remote northern Australia; and being chosen as the 2016 RMIT University Outstanding Alumnus Award Australia.

My belief in the concept of fate, the view that 'what will be, will be', was inherited from my grandmother and my mother. I consider that their fatalistic way of viewing the world was shaped by what life had dealt them. While I attribute my capacity to deal with change to my acceptance of the notion of fate, I did, however, realise at a young age that, while we may have little control over much of what happens around us, we have considerable power over how we will react to those events, encounters or situations. It was indeed fate that both my grandmother and my mother were born into a world where government policies directed that Aboriginal children could be removed from their families on the whim of one man, with the family, most often the mother of the child, having no rights in the matter whatsoever. It could also be argued that it was fate that led to my mother and her two sisters being physically removed from the comfort and security of living with their mother and brothers. But it was not fate that led to my mother and her two sisters being raised in an institution that not only separated them from the rest of their family by an insurmountable geographical distance, but also subjected them to the sort of treatment that led my mother to shut down her emotions and refuse to revisit her childhood for over 50 years.

Haebich, in her book *Broken Circles: Fragmenting Indigenous Families 1800–2000*, cites the *Bringing Them Home Report* to highlight the 'commonality of children's institutional experience across Australia' (2000, p. 345) despite their being 'accommodated in a range of institutions – mainstream child welfare homes, Aboriginal children's homes and segregated living areas referred to as compounds or dormitories within larger multipurpose Aboriginal institutions' (2000, p. 344). She describes how, depending on the type of institution in which they had been placed, Aboriginal children could not only be 'totally cut off from Aboriginal adults', but also, in some situations, such as those at the Bomaderry Infants Home, were "cut off from the rest of the world" (Haebich 2000, p. 346). My mother described to me how, apart from those Sundays when they were marched to and from church, they saw nothing of the outside world because the institution they were housed in was surrounded by a six-foot high corrugated iron fence. Their teachers, three older women, came daily to teach them. Once a year, usually near Christmas, the trustees presided over what was seen as a real treat, the annual picnic. My mother was raised in an institution in metropolitan Perth but she may as well have been raised in a prison far from civilisation, for these children were not even permitted to look at the outside world, to learn about life through visual imagery, as well as being denied contact with their own families. It is one thing to talk about institutionalisation but I had never envisaged the walls. From the age of six years, my mother (along with her older and younger sisters and many other children) was essentially imprisoned by the state. For days after she told me, all I could ask myself was 'Why? What had these children done to deserve being sent to prison?' Of course they, these little children, had done nothing – but they had to be rendered invisible so the 'outcomes' of government policies of the day could continue to remain unseen, and therefore ignored, by the wider population.

It has taken me many years to come to grips with that reality, to even begin to comprehend what that must have done to my mother and aunts in terms of their emotional wellbeing. The consequence of such deliberate treatment by the authorities was that, for most of her life, my mother experienced a deep sense of powerlessness as an Aboriginal woman. So much so that, as we, her daughters, were growing into adolescence, she made a point of telling us whenever she was discriminated against. I suspect she did this as a means of preparing us for whatever might lie ahead. I also believe, however, that the deep pain she suffered as a result of such discrimination was a critical factor in enabling her to make the decisions she later made about her children and their futures. Just as she did not leave our futures to fate, she also ensured we had some capacity to make more informed decisions about our future lives than she had been able to make about hers. In fact, we were raised from an early age to have some agency in our own decision-making. Her oft-repeated assertion, 'I know you will have done your best and that is all I ask of you!', was virtually her mantra for reminding us of our personal responsibility in whatever we were doing. I recognised that reality from an early age and believe it was quintessential to my capacity to deal with the often onerous responsibilities placed on me as the 'oldest' in the family. Accepting that there are circumstances over which we have no control, such as our place in the family, enables us not only to accept our reality but also to learn from the experience.

In thinking about how my early life has influenced the way I view the world, I must acknowledge the enduring influence of my family. Living up to the expectations implicit in being the oldest child may be difficult but I believe I benefited greatly from the experience. I know that accepting the responsibilities that were placed on me at a very early age enabled me to become highly independent. In having parents who were devoted to one another and to their children, I learned the value of strong relationships built on a foundation of love and respect, and gained a marker for my own life. Furthermore, I consider those qualities of communication and connection were strengthened through my position as 'first-born' in a large family, making a positive contribution to my capacity to engage effectively with others, either personally or professionally.

In the 1980s I spent some weeks in Kakadu, where I was fortunate enough to meet the Gagadju Elder and traditional owner Big Bill Neidjie. Through our many conversations about his feelings for his country, this very articulate man enabled me to understand my own sense of belonging in relation to the Kimberley. I align myself closely with Heaney's notion that while a sense of place can be intensely personal, a focal point for the individual, this stance can merge into 'thoughts of membership in social groups, of participation in activities that transcend the concerns of particular people, of close involvements with whole communities and their endearing historical traditions' (cited in Basso 1996, p. 85) – in other words, it can become a holistic force. Basso argues:

> *Fueled by sentiments of inclusion, belonging, and connectedness to the past, sense of place roots individuals in the social and cultural soils from which they have sprung together, holding them there in the grip of a shared identity, a localized version of selfhood.* (Basso 1996, p. 85)

Thus, in accepting that, to some degree, my sense of inclusion and belonging is attributable to the family environment in which I was reared, I also perceive that my strong sense of connectedness evolved out of my immersion in place as much as in family. This notion of shared identity has enabled me to develop the empathy that is an important characteristic of my effectiveness as a communicator in a diversity of personal and professional situations. My childhood experiences provided me with a solid foundation on which to build my career for they ensured that I developed many of the skills needed to be a good organiser, a manager, a teacher, a communicator, a leader. Importantly, those same experiences also gave me the capacity to participate, to engage collaboratively, to appreciate the importance of belonging.

My grandmother's special influence on me began at a young age when she would arrive, unannounced, to take my brother and myself out bush with her or to drive the entire family to Derby for time with the extended family. We didn't always want to go bush but we had no choice. In reflection, I realise such events were part of the building blocks of family discipline, an important lesson in learning to respect our elders. They represented a framework for self-discipline, enabling us to operate effectively within the cultural mores of family, community and, ultimately, the wider society. Such discipline enabled me to cope with the many changes that occurred in my life. I faced the first major change in my life when I was 12 years old and was sent south to high school. That first year was very difficult. Knowing there was no money for fares home during the year, the death of my father, three months after I left home, ushered in one of the loneliest and most miserable periods of my life, separated as I was from my family. My life had changed forever – I was desperately lonely and now, for the first time in my life, I felt I was on my own. Financial poverty was a reality of life for us, but from an early age we learned to share everything – from the food on the table to the good times, the sad times and the in-between times. We played (and fought) with one another, stood up for one another, learned to respect one another and, most importantly, we were encouraged to depend upon and love one another. And when my grandmother took us out bush, we ranged across vast areas of the Kimberley, meeting up with family, experiencing our country, engaging with our heritage. It was this childhood that instilled my sense of identity as an Aboriginal person, 'connected' me with the extended family and imbued my strong sense of place, of belonging, of being grounded. I would argue that it is this sense of belonging that empowers us to make the connections that allow us to grow and move forward while also creating the pathways that enable us to move in and out of each other's reality. I know that this capacity to connect has been a powerful influence in enabling me to be a 'good' teacher.

My mother was a powerful role model for me. She went out to work and through dint of much scratching and saving, and finding all the scholarships or bursaries we could access, she sent every one of her children away to secondary school. Her commitment to education and what it could offer her children in terms of improving our lot in life has been a lifelong inspiration to me. Just how much has become very evident in my own life. Following the death of my husband when our sons were aged 11 years and nine years, I committed myself to ensuring they received the quality education that we had planned for them. This was not always easy but, as my mother before me, I was determined that my children would have the education they needed to pursue the career they wanted for themselves. I continue to believe that education is the greatest gift you can give your children.

My mother always had an air of aloofness, a private person who kept herself to herself. But, in her late sixties, on a visit home, I convinced her to talk to me about her childhood – what was it like being raised in the home, how did the experience influence her life, how did she feel about it now, half a century later? She was extremely reluctant to talk, falling back on the excuse she had always used when, as young children, we would ask her to tell us what she used to do when she was a kid, and she would simply respond 'some things are best forgotten'. But I was persistent and finally she relented. It took the best part of three days, just the two of us and many 'cuppas'. Over most of the first day she talked about her earliest memories, especially memories of Derby and neighbouring families. I continued bringing her back to herself and, finally, she began. It was as though I had opened the floodgates and the memories just overflowed. By the end of the third day, I sensed she was exhausted. I suggested she might like to talk about how she felt right now. She was silent for so long I thought she might not be able to take this final step, but then the pain and rage she had kept locked deep inside for all those years finally broke out and she spat out the words: 'Slaves, that's what they educated us for – just to be slaves!' I had never seen my mother so angry and I finally understood the depth of her pain. My only regret was that I hadn't done this many years before so that she could have enjoyed a few more years of freedom from the past.

Reflecting on Indigenous women's intellectual traditions, in terms of the influences that shaped us, that made us who we are today, I would argue that it is impossible to ignore the historical experience. For Australia's First Peoples, this became a continuous struggle for survival. In thinking about the lives of my grandmother, my mother and myself, I acknowledge that, while each of us may have lived during different eras, we shared common life experiences. I believe it was those connections that influenced the way in which we thought, the knowledge we acquired and the values and beliefs we adhered to. Our capacity to adapt to isolation was not only a product of being raised in a sparsely populated, remote, often harsh, geographic landscape. It was also the result of an endless struggle to exist in a society shaped by successive government policies that, clearly demonstrated a total disregard for Aboriginal peoples. It was the establishment of this framework for institutional racism (Eckermann 1992, p. 31) that almost decimated this country's Indigenous peoples. But an alternative reality could be that this commonality of historical experience strengthened family bonds and contributed to the persistence that has enabled us to overcome oppression and take control of our own lives.

In writing about their own families, Aboriginal writers such as Ruby Langford Ginibi, Sally Morgan, Jackie Huggins and Pat Dudgeon have provided critical insights into the way in which many Indigenous women have assumed an increasingly important role in maintaining and nurturing their family units and ultimately ensuring the survival of their families and cultural identity in a rapidly changing world. In my opinion, it has been through the persistence of Indigenous women such as my grandmother and my mother – incredibly strong, determined individuals – that we have been able to recapture enough of the past to create a strong foundation upon which Indigenous Australians will be able to build a better future for themselves and their families. This notion of 'recapturing' the past is a critical one for, while we cannot physically experience something that has happened in the past, we can, if we know the stories and remember the events that happened, be guided by that knowledge. It is a matter of understanding that 'Wisdom sits in places' (Basso 1996, p. 67). It is our responsibility as Indigenous women to ensure the knowledge of the past reveals the truth that Indigenous Australian women in this country are not a homogeneous group, rather the diversity of their vastly different cultural backgrounds, and the wisdom that is a part of their legacies, has added a richly dynamic dimension to all our lives. In using our connections with place to pass on the wisdom, we can ensure those memories of the past will contribute to the building of a collective capacity that will enable us to work together to ensure a better future becomes the reality for our peoples.

Family is what lies at the heart of Indigenous Australian society. Research designed to identify the issues that maintain the deficit positioning of Indigenous Australians within the wider Australian society has highlighted the importance of culture by providing deeper insights into the possible origins of much contemporary practice (Dudgeon et al. 2012; Herbert and Gilbert 2005). Despite the fracturing of Indigenous cultures that occurred through the colonisation process in this country, remnants of traditional cultural practices persist. The modern Indigenous family is often an extended family that carries a range of responsibilities with it. For instance, many of us continue to share responsibilities for our children, especially where someone dies and another sibling takes responsibility for growing up that person's children and/or grandchildren.

Significantly, in modern families, the greatest share of responsibility for 'growing up' children often falls on women as colonisation has imposed different cultural interpretations around the traditional woman's role in Indigenous communities. While the task of raising children premised on the values of respect, reciprocity and responsibility has never been easy, it has acquired additional complexities where women are also struggling to meet the demands of full-time work or study or both. One of the most critical aspects of Indigenous women's lives is the practice of looking outwards, beyond the self, in order to put family and community first. Implicit in accepting the responsibility for nurturing both family and community is the need to remain in touch with individuals and/or groups, to demonstrate commitment through one's own ongoing engagement. My mother's continual focus on her family, in particular her own children, was, I would argue, engendered by her own childhood experiences. And my commitment to focusing firstly on my own family and then on the communities that exist within the context of Indigenous education, reflects the influences of my life experiences and, subsequently, my learning journey in education.

My own educational experiences enabled me to appreciate not only the importance of education but also the value of achievement. I used my PhD research to examine Indigenous notions of success in the context of the

Australian university. In reflecting on the findings of this study I realised that the experiences of the students I had interviewed were often closely aligned with my own experiences, hence they served to reinforce my own concepts around the value of education. For example, in arguing that their studies had given them skills that have made them more open minded and flexible in their thinking, challenged them to want to insert themselves into academic discourses, and made them feel they could make their own choices, the student informants were indicating that they felt competent to operate within Western knowledge frameworks (Herbert 2003, p. 257). More importantly, however, combined with their revelations concerning their personal growth in terms of cultural identity, these qualities could be seen as evidence of their competence to operate within both, or either, Western and Indigenous frameworks. These students were seeking to create new discourses rather than simply engaging at the interface to buy into the discourses of the other. In moving from the margins of the university towards the centre, they were developing the potential to change the Western historical model and beginning to articulate what it was that they wanted from the university (Herbert 2003, p. 258).

The issue of 'identity' and its perceived importance in relation to Indigenous performance emerged as a critical factor in my research for it became obvious that identity, since the colonial era, had been used as a tool of oppression. Ironically, it would seem that it may now serve to enhance Indigenous students' capacity to succeed in the contemporary world because Indigenous Australians have, over decades, been made aware of their difference and had to develop strategies that enable them to cope with difference and to operate within a diversity of lifestyles (Herbert 2003, p. 68). Many Indigenous Australians have, therefore, developed a particular strength in the cultural competencies which are essential to operating effectively within a modern society while still maintaining critical connections with their own cultural milieu. Bird Rose (1998, p. 34), in describing her time with Aboriginal people in the field, said: 'I am led into a world of connection and responsibility ... Care of one's country, one's people, one's Dreaming sites, and one's non-human countrymen are just some of the actions which people engage in as part of living powerfully in the world'. This implies an overwhelming sense of the power that emanates from people living harmoniously and responsibly within their environment. Such insights into the potential of cross-cultural interaction pose serious ontological and epistemological questions for Australian universities and their continuing failure to value Indigenous intellectual traditions. Dudgeon and colleagues (1998, p. 5) warned almost two decades ago that, 'we need to be careful that claims made in terms of the 'common good' do not become a justification for silencing voices of groups that are only just starting to be heard'.

Contemporary literature is evidence that Indigenous peoples are beginning to speak for themselves, through their research and writing, and that a growing number of women have become powerful voices for their people. And publications such as this book clearly demonstrate that Indigenous writers are engaging in the discourse in their own right, taking up the challenge to move Indigenous knowledge from the margins into the mainstream of academic debate. In encouraging Indigenous Australian authors to engage in a process that allows First Nations cultures to emerge:

> *We seek to minimise the influence of the 'master narratives' – the theories and perspectives of non-Aboriginal academics – which tend to dominate writing in books such as this. We claim the right to speak in our own voice, to have that voice accepted as legitimate and authentic, and, in the process, to minimise the likelihood that our experience will be colonised by other interpretations of our own experience.* (Dudgeon et al. 1996: 32)

While the purpose of this book was to enable a number of Indigenous Australian women to share with 'non-Aboriginal academics' (Dudgeon et al. 1996) their ideas and thinking on a range of issues associated with identity and representation, it is equally important to recognise such engagement as a critical dimension in their growth as individuals. In reflecting on what to share of their own life experiences and how, writers must guard against the dangers of 'solipsism' or one-selfism that Fay (1996, p. 9) warned could adversely influence an insider's capacity for objective interpretation of the data they are sharing with others. It is vital that, in interpreting our own lived experience in the context of how such experience might reveal the academic traditions that have shaped us, we are aware we are operating from within our own epistemology and need to acknowledge that,

> *The answer lies in distinguishing knowing from being. I may be myself but this doesn't mean that I therefore know myself. Knowing an experience doesn't just mean having it: it means being able to say what it is (in some*

> *broad sense which includes both discursive and non-discursive expressions). Knowledge consists not in the experience itself but in grasping the sense of this experience. For this reason knowledge is not psychic identification but interpretive understanding: knowing ourselves and others is an instance of decoding, classifying, and explicating rather than an instance of psychic union.* (Fay 1996, p. 28)

When I am invited to speak, I have to first decide the position from which I speak. It is only in knowing who I represent that the 'real' me can begin to say what needs to be said, within the particular context. The 'real' me can then interpret the sense of my life and learning experiences and the essential meaning derived from those experiences, so that others might translate the inferred meaning and better understand the voice they are hearing. It is the intellectual traditions and learning experiences I have acquired through my life that have enabled me to know who I am as an Aboriginal woman, thus enabling the 'real' me to stand up when needed.

BIBLIOGRAPHY

Basso, KH (1996) 'Wisdom sits in places: notes on a western Apache landscape', in S Feld and KH Basso (eds), *Senses of Place*, School of American Research Advanced Seminar Series, New Mexico, pp. 53–90.

Bird Rose, D (1998) 'Social justice, ecological justice, reconciliation', in L Manderson (ed.), *Reconciliation: Voices from the Academy*, Academy of the Social Sciences, Canberra.

Dudgeon, P, Oxenham, D and Grogan, G (1996) 'Learning identities and differences', in C Luke (ed.), *Feminisms and Pedagogies of Everyday Life,* State University of New York Press, Albany, pp. 31–55.

Dudgeon, P, Abdullah, J, Humphries, R and Walker, R (1998) 'Social capital and increasing Aboriginal participation in mainstream courses: weaving the threads of the social fabric or spinning another yarn?', in R Walker, D Elliott, K Seymour and G Worby (eds), *Indigenous Education and the Social Capital Conference. Influences on the Performance of Indigenous Tertiary Students*, Black Swan Press, Adelaide.

Dudgeon, P, Cox, K, D'Anna, D, Dunkley, C, Hams, K, Kelly, K, Scrine, C and Walker, R (2012) *Hear our Voices: Community Consultations for the Development of an Empowerment, Healing and Leadership Program for Aboriginal People Living in the Kimberley, Western Australia,* Final research report, Commonwealth of Australia, Canberra.

Eckermann, A-K (1992) *Binan Goonj: Bridging Cultures in Aboriginal Health*, University of New England Press, Armidale.

Fay, B (1996) *Contemporary Philosophy of Social Science: A Multicultural Approach*, Blackwell Publishers, Cambridge, MA.

Haebich, A (2000) *Broken Circles: Fragmenting Indigenous Families 1800–2000*, Fremantle Arts Centre Press, Fremantle.

Haebich, A and Reece, RHW (1988) 'Neville, Auber Octavius (1875–1954)', *Australian Dictionary of Biography*, Australian National University, viewed 20 August 2016, <http://adb.anu.edu.au/biography/neville-auber-octavius-7821>.

Herbert, HJ (2003) 'Is success a matter of choice? Exploring Indigenous Australian notions of success within the context of the Australian university', PhD thesis, RMIT University, Melbourne.

Herbert, J and Gilbert, R (2005) *Indigenous Boys' Module*, Success For Boys Professional Learning Programme, Curriculum Corporation, James Cook University, viewed 20 August 2016, <http://researchonline.jcu.edu.au/28096/>.

HREOC (Human Rights and Equal Opportunity Commission) (1997) *Bringing Them Home Report*, Commonwealth of Australia, Sydney.

Smith, LT (2001) *Decolonizing Methodologies: Research and Indigenous Peoples*, Zed Books and University of Otago Press, London and Dunedin.

AMBELIN KWAYMULLINA belongs to the Palyku people from the Pilbara, in the north-west of Western Australia. She is an Indigenous lawyer, writer and illustrator, currently employed at the University of Western Australia.

THE CREATORS OF THE FUTURE: WOMEN, LAW AND TELLING STORIES IN COUNTRY

Ambelin Kwaymullina

> *We are Women. We are not victims. Nor are we merely survivors. We are Women. We have creation powers. We are the Creators of the Future.*
> Judy Atkinson of the Jiman and Bundjalung peoples (2002, p. 3)

THE STORY OF CROW AND THE WATERHOLE

There once was a Crow who lived in a tree by a waterhole.

Crow was unhappy. Each morning, she stared into the water, and saw another crow staring back. Crow thought Crow-in-the-waterhole was the most wonderful bird she had ever seen. 'She looks like a crow who could change the world. I wish I could be like her.'

This went on until, finally, Crow flew away to seek her destiny, hoping to become as wonderful as Crow-in-the-waterhole. Crow had not flown far when the air grew hot and she heard the crackle of flames. Looking down, she saw fire racing across the ground towards a tiny green gum tree. 'Please help me, Crow!' cried Little

Gum. 'One day I will be a big tree where crows can make their nests. But now I am small and the fire will burn me up.'

Crow was very afraid of fire. But, remembering how much she loved her own tree by the waterhole, she launched herself downwards to pull Little Gum from the ground. She carried him until she found a river surrounded by many trees, and placed him gently on the earth. 'Thank you, Crow!' called Little Gum, happily digging his roots into the soil.

But Crow was unhappy, for in the river she saw a crow even more wonderful than Crow-in-the-waterhole. 'She looks like a crow that is very brave. I wish I could be like her.'

And Crow flew on, sadly.

Crow heard someone calling her from below. Looking down, she saw a young goanna clinging to the side of a rock pool. 'Crow, Crow!' cried Goanna. 'I went to get a drink but I fell in! Can you pull me out?'

Crow saw that the sides of the pool were not steep, and Goanna, though young, was big and strong. 'Goanna,' Crow called, 'You're such a fine, large goanna, I know you can climb out on your own.'

Crow sounded so sure of this that Goanna believed her, and with a mighty heave, he hauled himself out of the water. 'Thank you, Crow!' called Goanna, skittering happily away. But Crow was unhappy, for in the rock pool she saw a crow even more wonderful that Crow-in-the-river or Crow-in-the-waterhole. 'She looks like a crow that has great faith in others. I wish I could be like her.'

And Crow flew on, sadder than ever.

Soon dark clouds filled the sky. Lightning flashed, thunder roared, and it began to rain. Crow saw a paperbark tree standing all alone, and plunged downwards to shelter in its branches. 'Oh, Crow!' cried Paperbark. 'You are my first visitor in such a long time. I was burned in a fire and lost all my leaves. Now I have grown back bushier than ever, but all the animals have forgotten me. Can you sing to remind them I am here?'

Crow didn't like to sing, because the other birds teased her about her harsh voice. But she felt sorry for Paperbark, so when the storm passed she flew around and around, calling loudly,

'Caw! Caw! Caw! Poor Paperbark, all alone! Come see Paperbark, all strong and green! Caw! Caw!'

Crow's voice carried a long way and animals began to follow the sound. Ants marched, lizards crawled and birds flew until all of Paperbark was filled with life. 'Thank you, Crow!' called Paperbark, rustling his branches happily.

But Crow was unhappy, for in a puddle left by the rain she saw a crow even more wonderful than Crow-in-the-pool, Crow-in-the-river or Crow-in-the-waterhole. 'She looks like a crow with a kind heart. I wish I could be like her.'

And this time Crow was so sad that she began to cry.

A kookaburra flapped down to land beside her. 'Crow, why are you crying?' he asked. 'The sun is bright and all the animals have come back to Paperbark! What's there to be sad about?'

So Crow told Kookaburra about how she had left her home to seek her destiny, but that everywhere she went she kept seeing other crows, each more wonderful than the last. 'Oh, Kookaburra!' she sobbed. 'How can I ever be as good as any of them?'

Kookaburra laughed and laughed. 'Silly Crow! Crow-in-the-waterhole is you, and Crow-in-the-river is you, and Crow-in-the-pool is you, and Crow-in-the-puddle is you! You have been looking at your own reflection all along.'

Crow stared at Kookaburra, and then at the puddle. She touched the water with her beak, and when Crow-in-the-puddle rippled and disappeared, she realised she had indeed been staring at her own image.

Happy at last, Crow returned to her tree by the waterhole. But this time, when she looked into the water, she saw a crow that was brave, faithful, kind and wise, and she knew that the crow was her.

In the years that followed, whenever Crow met someone seeking their destiny, she would show them their reflection in the waterhole, and say – 'Your destiny lies within you. All you need to do is learn how to see it.'

Ambelin Kwaymullina

Indigenous women are part of an ancient tradition of storytelling. We have long told the creation tales of how life was made, through dance and song, art and poetry, and a multitude of other forms of narrative. These tales teach us not just how the world began, but also how to live so that the world always continues. Our stories are not separate or separated from us – narrative lived in the land and was woven into every facet of our existence. Our stories are still in our lands and in ourselves. But now not all of them are tales of creation. Since the coming of the colonisers, we have inherited a different kind of narrative that tells of death, dispossession and destruction. These stories, too, are now part of us and of our country.

In a still colonial world, we as Indigenous women must negotiate our way through structures, institutions and workspaces that are not reflective of Aboriginal worldviews; manage multiple responsibilities to family and to country; and deal with the complex effects of multigenerational trauma upon ourselves, our families and our homelands. As my mother often says, Indigenous people walk in many different worlds – and before us is the challenge of creating a positive future for those who are yet to come. What stories can we as women now tell to ourselves and to our children that will enable us to value our holistic Indigenous selves? That will equip us to perceive and sustain the connections between people and people, and people and country, which have always been the core of an Indigenous way of being? And that have allowed us to so far overcome the devastation of colonialism so that we can imagine the possibility of a better world for ourselves and for future generations of Indigenous people?

WOMEN, DREAMING AND COUNTRY

The many countries of the many Aboriginal nations of Australia were formed by the creative Ancestors in the Dreaming. Aboriginal peoples never told a tale in which a single man made the world, or even one in which a single human did. We tell of a world formed by male and female, by human and crow and snake and goanna and a multitude of other shapes of life. The women of the Indigenous nations of this continent were born along with grandmother crow and sister rock, formed out of the substance of the earth, our mother. We began here thousands upon thousands of years ago and, from the beginning, Indigenous women were women of power. We walked the hills and the riverbanks and the deserts; we cared for the sacred places;

and we followed the law that gave us a place that was different from, but not inferior to, that of the men.

Before the Ancestors came, the world was shapeless, a place without form or meaning. It was the Ancestors who made not just the forms of life, but life itself. I have previously written of this as a pattern that is stable but not fixed, and has many threads of many colours (Kwaymullina 2005, p. 13). Every thread is connected to, and therefore has a relationship with, all the others. The individual threads are every shape of life. Some, like those recognised to be human, kangaroo, paperbark tree, are known to Western science as 'alive'; others, like rock, would be called 'non-living'. But rock is there, just the same. Human is there, too, though it is neither the most nor the least important thread – it is one among many, equal with the others. The pattern made by the whole is in each thread and all the threads together make the whole. Stand close to the pattern and you can focus on a single thread; stand a little further back and you can see how that thread connects to others; stand further back still and you can see it all – and it is only once you see it all that you can recognise the pattern of the whole in every individual thread. The whole is more than its parts and the whole is in all its parts. This is the pattern that the Ancestors made. It is life, creation, spirit, and it exists in country.

The pattern created in the Dreaming is what forms and informs all life. But, being life, this pattern is dynamic and so must be sustained and renewed if it is to continue. That is why there is law, to show how to live in the world in a way that sustains the world.

Indigenous women now exist within social realities that often speak of the need for work-life balance. But for generations of Indigenous women, there was no 'work' that was not itself a part of living and a part of renewing the life in others. When women moved through the country gathering food, we walked the trails that the Ancestors had walked and we sang the songs that told the stories of those Ancestors, the stories of country. We took only certain foods, at certain times, in certain quantities. Our journeys – far from the random, nomadic wanderings of the European imagination – were ones of purpose, of teaching, of celebration and of caring for country. Our 'work' was a task that sustained and renewed ourselves, our connections to each other and the connections between women and country. The whole is more than its parts and the whole is in all its parts. This is what it was, and is, to live holistically in a holistic reality.

WOMEN, DISPOSSESSION AND COUNTRY

When the British came to Australia, they were ill-equipped to understand or even to perceive the holistic reality that was so clear to Indigenous people and so central to Indigenous existence. The systems the English brought with them were patriarchal and hierarchical, informed by a belief in the inherent superiority of the male gender and the Caucasian race. Their science told them that the whole was never more than the sum of its measurable parts, and their religion spoke of the sacred as something to be found in heaven and not in earth. Neither their men nor their women recognised the mother in the earth, the grandmother in the crow or the sister in the rock, and because they valued their own worldview above all others, they did not listen to the peoples who might have told them otherwise. Instead, they sought to impose their own fragmented and fragmenting perspective upon Indigenous peoples and Indigenous country.

The two centuries that followed the arrival of the British were times of devastation for the women of country, of death and disease, of slavery and stolen children, and damage to the connections between people and people, and people and country, from which women drew their sustenance, their safety and their strength. The shattering experience of colonialism in turn shattered Indigenous female identity, fragmenting the holistic way of being that had sustained Indigenous women in country for so many thousands of years.

INDIGENOUS WOMEN AND THE CREATION OF THE FUTURE

In the wake of colonialism, the damaged and broken connections between people and people, and people and country, mean that – like Crow – we can sometimes struggle to see our world and ourselves clearly. We are susceptible, as all inheritors of trauma are susceptible, to assigning ourselves too little value. The consequences of this extend far beyond our own lives to affect not only others around us, but also the life of the world itself.

The essence of holistic living is to recognise the whole in all that we are and all that we do. This means that everything and anything we do must begin with first perceiving, and then valuing, the Indigenous whole within us. In the pressures of living in a colonial nation-state, this can be a difficult task. We can struggle with persistent stereotypes of Indigenous identity and with negative myths about Indigenous existence generated by the West. We can become overwhelmed with a multitude of responsibilities and allow ourselves to become trapped in the role of being the continual helper: the person who gives to others at the expense of themselves. But Crow teaches us that if we do not nurture the whole within ourselves, then we cannot nurture it in anyone else. When we don't value ourselves enough as people, as women, we lose the ability to accurately assess the strengths and weaknesses of others, and we reduce, rather than enhance, our ability to do good in the world. We make compromises when we do not need to and we give our power away to those who will not use it as generously or as wisely as we would. The Crow story itself is one that came to me in a time of great sadness when I doubted my own power. I dreamed the entire story and I have always believed that it was a gift from the old grandmothers, who knew how much I needed to hear the message of the tale.

Any failure to see worth in ourselves as Indigenous people means we also fail to see the worth in our own ways of being, making it difficult for us to follow our own path when those around us place value on a different way of knowing the world. We are daily challenged to assert our holistic Indigenous self as we negotiate our way through Western spaces and ways of being that remain heavily influenced by reductionism. But even Western knowledge systems are coming to recognise the value of a more holistic perspective – and the very first thing that anyone reduces with a reductionist perspective is themselves. If we live our lives dividing things into smaller and smaller categories, and failing to see the connections between those categories, we lose our ability to view ourselves as whole people. We assign ourselves roles, or allow others to assign them to us, and these roles come with expectations that we then feel we must meet. And because we cannot see the whole within ourselves, we have no hope of seeing it in others, or in the world, of perceiving how it is that we are all connected – to ourselves, to each other and to all other life.

Indigenous women today are the inheritors of the multigenerational trauma of dispossession. But we are also the inheritors of a much older and more enduring legacy. We are born of the red desert sand, the shining blue sea and the ancient spirit of this country. And although we have suffered terrible damage as a people and a culture, the essence of our holistic identity remains embedded in this living land. The reflection of our whole selves is all around us, if we can only learn how to perceive and value it. And in so doing, we can help to create a future where life within ourselves, and all around us, is nurtured and made whole.

BIBLIOGRAPHY

Atkinson, J (2002) *Trauma Trails, Recreating Song Lines: The Transgenerational Effects of Trauma in Indigenous Australia*, Spinifex Press, Melbourne.

Kwaymullina, A (2005) 'Seeing the light: Aboriginal law, learning and sustainable living in country', *Indigenous Law Bulletin*, vol. 6, no. 11, pp. 12–16.

Kwaymullina, A (2007) *Crow and the Waterhole*, Fremantle Press, Fremantle.

PROFESSOR PAT DUDGEON is from the Bardi people of the Kimberley area in Western Australia. She is a psychologist and research fellow at the School of Indigenous Studies at the University of Western Australia. Her area of research includes Indigenous social and emotional wellbeing and suicide prevention. Amongst her many commitments, she is a commissioner of the Australian National Mental Health Commission, deputy chair of the Australian Indigenous Psychologists Association, chair of the National Aboriginal Torres Strait Islander Leaders Mental Health and co-chair of the ministerial Aboriginal Torres Strait Islander Mental Health and Suicide Prevention Advisory Group. She is currently the director of the National Empowerment Project, an Indigenous suicide prevention project working with 11 sites in Aboriginal communities across the country and the Aboriginal and Torres Strait Islander Suicide Prevention Evaluation Project. She is actively involved with the Aboriginal community and has a commitment to social justice for Indigenous people.

MOTHERS OF SIN: INDIGENOUS WOMEN'S PERCEPTIONS OF THEIR IDENTITY AND GENDER

Pat Dudgeon

The histories of my foremothers and many Aboriginal women are stories of endurance and resilience as much as they may be stories of the rapes, indignities and prejudice suffered. Their resistance and survival fills our hearts with respect, pride and admiration. Our responsibility is to ensure that their stories, so often silenced, are remembered through oral histories and through other kinds of texts. When we retell their lives, it is a tribute to all those women who endured so much oppression; who had their lands taken; who were dislocated into missions, reserves and other Western institutions to be controlled and dictated to; who were given to understand that their culture was primitive; who endured and fought back in ways that they could. This chapter focuses on the ways Aboriginal women have resisted colonisation and oppression, the ways they fought back to protect themselves and their children – whether it was playing the game and playing humble or whether it was standing up and fighting the system.

This is a woman's story. This is a fighting story. It is a tribute to those women who bunched their skirts up into their gowich (underpants) so they could fight without encumbrance. They fought the system, and even their men and each other when necessary.

Aboriginal women's perceptions of identity, gender and sexuality are inextricably intertwined – and deeply rooted in the Australian colonising project. As women, they have suffered racism unlike white women; as Aboriginal women, they have suffered sexism unlike Aboriginal men; and they have suffered misperceptions of their traditional roles and misbeliefs that as women they are better off under the structures of Western colonisation. Aboriginal women's sexuality has been commodified – as the frontier expanded they were used for sexual services by white settlers, and yet viewed with contempt as sexual beings by white society. Despite this history of oppression, many Aboriginal women have maintained, then and now, a strong sense of themselves and their sexuality. Aboriginal women appreciate those women who have a grounded sense of themselves as women.

Two of those women were my grandmother, Martha, and her mother, Lillian. When I started reading about the social and historical context of their lives, I was grateful that I lived now as a woman and as an Aboriginal person. My grandmother and her mother lived through the times when the oppressive legislation of the Aborigines Act 1905 (Western Australia) was enforced in full upon Aboriginal people. Perhaps the only good that came from that Act was the detailed records of control and surveillance it produced. We can use these records to bear testimony to the oppression of the lives of earlier generations of our people.

My grandmother never talked about her oppression. She only spoke about the good times of her life. Perhaps it was impossible to speak the unspeakable and perhaps she thought speaking it would make others think that she was somehow deserving of the demeaning treatment meted out to her across her life. As Jackie Huggins wrote,

> *My mother does not want to talk even to me about the kinds of bitter treatment she experienced. What stops her from speaking is the same thing that stops other people speaking about the profound suffering they have experienced. The oppression and pain can be so fierce as to make people mute. They carry this experience inside themselves ... Guilt and shame are manifest in women who have suffered this and there is a self-blaming that makes them see their situations as their fault or the fault of their race.* (Huggins and Huggins 1994, p. 36)

So, telling my grandmother's story – a tale of resistance and resilience – is important. Many Aboriginal women have expressed not only admiration for our foremothers and their resistance but also a need to speak their stories, to speak up Aboriginal women's power and strength. Indigenous scholars have a sense of obligation to speak out to all the injustice that has been done to our people across many generations. In some senses, we are the generation that has had opportunities our mothers never had, and we have power and agency (albeit limited) that they never had.

Many people, even our own people, think that educated Aboriginal people or Aboriginal people who work in government do not know about racism and suffering, that somehow they are insulated. Maybe some of these privileged people might not have had to deal with poverty and despair as earlier generations have, but none that I know are insulated: we see the effects of disempowerment all around us in the drunkenness of our aunties, the imprisonment of our brothers, the suicides of our cousins, the sexual abuse in our families, the drug abuse, the 'lostness' and the despair. Strong, 'successful' Aboriginal women stand on the edge of the cliff, mindful of our own fears, weakness and frustrations, constantly checking to see if we are bringing about social change, keeping our families together, empowering our people. In different ways, no less was expected of our foremothers – different times call for different strengths. Through their stories and ours, we can name oppressions and injustices, we can name our strengths, culture and spirituality, and we can also celebrate how we as individuals had to, and still do, join together to make rich lives amid the difficulties.

THE SEXUAL EXPLOITATION OF INDIGENOUS WOMEN

The historical literature shows that Aboriginal people, especially the women, were considered by white society to be sexually permissive and easily available, and that Aboriginal groups would be contented as long as goods were exchanged for the sexual services of the women. Such perceptions may or may not have been conditioned by a European 'knowledge' of the accepted traditional Aboriginal practice of 'lending' or trading wives. Either way, the forcible abduction of Aboriginal women for sexual services is part of Australian history. The practice of kidnapping Aboriginal women was common and most conflicts between local Aboriginal groups and settlers was a consequence of the appropriation of women. Indeed, the widespread practice of stealing and exploiting Aboriginal women was described as a type of slave trade by contemporary observers of the late 1800s (Evans, et al. 1992). Aboriginal women were 'easy sport' within a colonial context.

As well as non-Aboriginal academics, many Aboriginal academics have written about this. Judy Atkinson (1990, p. 22) remarks that 'the invaders saw two things of value – the land and the women. One was seized for permanent possession; the other was used and discarded'. Larissa Behrendt comments:

> *The bodies of black women are contested terrain, the spoils of colonial conquest. Aboriginal women, who enjoyed power and respect within traditional communities, fell to the lowest rung on the socio-economic ladder in colonial society because of the double taint of a subordinated gender. Through this transferred misogyny many black men have been quick to learn that exploitation of black women was acceptable and quick to forget the status Aboriginal women held in their own communities.* (Behrendt 2000, p. 364)

Historian Susan Hunt examined the archives to look at the roles of women in the settlement expansion in northern Western Australia from 1860 to 1900, and concluded that, within the hardship and disadvantages for all women in the settlement of the north of the state, Aboriginal women were by far the most oppressed and disadvantaged:

> *Not only were Aboriginal women a source of cheap labour, but also they were treated by some European men as a sexual commodity. Miscegenation was widespread throughout northern Western Australia. In some instances, Aboriginal women may have gone willingly with Europeans and Asian men, but there is much evidence of force and abduction. Men often rationalised miscegenation by claiming that Aboriginal women were 'available' and irresistibly alluring.* (Hunt 1986, p. 104)

Hunt echoes the literature about Aboriginal women's experiences across the continent.

Aboriginal women were very aware of the perceptions of them as sexualised beings. In the Northern Territory, colloquial names for Aboriginal women indicated their objectification and the lack of agency they suffered. These names included 'studs', 'clean skins', 'spinifex fairies' and 'pandanus fairies' (McGrath 1987). When I was growing up in Darwin in the 1970s, derogatory terms, including all of these, were commonplace names for Aboriginal women who had sexual relations with white men. These women were considered 'easy' and animalistic, called 'gins' and 'black velvet', and the men who had relations with them were held in contempt, referred to as 'gin burglars' and 'gin jockeys'.

HISTORICAL PERCEPTIONS: SILENCING INDIGENOUS WOMEN

To understand the stories of our foremothers (and our own stories), we need to understand not only the sexual commodification of Aboriginal women, but also the dual influences of racist and sexist ideologies on how they were perceived. The poignant probability is that internalisation of such brutal perceptions resulted in the silencing of Aboriginal women's views of themselves and their worlds.

An example of dominant male views influencing perceptions of the role of Aboriginal women is in *I, the Aboriginal* by Douglas Lockwood. First published in 1962, this is the story of an Alawa man, Waipuldanya, told in the first person. Although the text would be considered old-fashioned and patronising nowadays, for its time and audience the book was useful for attempting to provide cross-cultural understandings of an Aboriginal worldview. It made sense of and fostered the value of certain Aboriginal cultural activities by comparing them to European practices. These white, middle-class analogies were mediated through Douglas's thoughts presented as Waipuldanya's. Glaring gender biases are typified in the description of Waipuldanya's mother:

> *She was a human being, female but unfeminine, unadorned, perhaps unattractive, but the only kind of woman who could share the life of a nomad. She did not feel the need for the fripperies I have seen some Aboriginal women wearing today. She was entirely subservient to her husband, my father Barnabas – a chattel, an incubator for his sons, her role ordered for her by the dictatorship of the tribe according to the inflexible sociological pattern.* (Lockwood 1980 [1962], p. 8)

After some discussion about the low status of Aboriginal women, including disparaging the secret Digga ceremony of the women, Lockwood concludes, somewhat irrelevantly, that,

> *The originator of the phrase 'never underestimate the power of a woman', was thinking of people other than the aborigines, perhaps the matriarchal*

> *Polynesians who crawled before important women on their hands and knees.* (1980, p. 128)

These comments about Aboriginal women represent Lockwood's anxious Western male view of the world. Effectively contemptuous of the notion of revering women of colour (Aboriginal or Polynesian or Asian), he failed to see any similarity between the matriarchs of these cultures and the respect accorded to queens and female nobility in Western cultures. This text, which on its publication became 'an Australian classic', is representative of the prevailing social thought towards different cultures and, especially, the position of Aboriginal women in mid twentieth-century Australia.

Settler stories like this, which I grew up with, had me believe that, as an Aboriginal woman, I should be grateful that I lived in a Western world rather than in a traditional Aboriginal context. Even an Aboriginal male colleague, with whom I was discussing gender issues, said, 'Yeah, how would you like it if you were living in the old times and had to marry some greasy old man, all you black women baulk at that!' With great creativity and gusto, he went into dramatic and enthusiastic description of an imagined lecherous old man slobbering over my person and expected me to react with repugnance. I paused to think and replied that I would be socialised into thinking that this was acceptable; such an arrangement would be endorsed by the community and the old husband would look after me, and I might even have other lovers should I choose.

Settlers' stories in part have become our stories, and new directions in the academy do not filter down immediately and uniformly. It is a concern how the distorted depictions and perceptions influence our thinking. As Maori academic Linda Tuhiwai Smith (1999) insisted, Indigenous people must challenge and critique every story and all knowledges about us to ensure we decolonise our minds and rebuild our contemporary cultures in strong, powerful ways. From an Indigenous viewpoint, history and received knowledge are contested areas for both are products of the colonising projects of the West. Thus, a defining project for us is to contest, challenge and critique such knowledges and histories. This concern is supported by postcolonial discourses that work not only in the academy, but also on the street to enable all of us – Indigenous and non-Indigenous Australians, men and women, to challenge the master narratives and to traverse the boundaries between them. Indigenous topics do not make up one discrete discipline but by nature are located in many disciplines and thereby need to be addressed through the range of different perspectives and discourses. Further, individuals cannot be understood in isolation from personal histories, families, broader communities, reference groups and the collective histories of societies, nor in isolation from an understanding of the meanings, ideologies, power relationships and cultures of societies, and how we participate in sustaining them even as they act to define us (Wetherell 1996; Wetherell et al. 1998).

Martha's story has a time and place. The place was Broome, Western Australia, from about the 1930s to World War II – a booming pearling town with a large number of Asian people, mainly men, who were indentured labourers on the pearling luggers. They came from China, Japan, Malaya, Timor, the Philippines, the Torres Strait Islands and Sri Lanka. It was a melting pot of different cultures, a multicultural town with people from a variety of different countries. Aboriginal people were the lowest on the social ladder (Edwards 1984).

Another place was Beagle Bay Mission, north of Broome in the West Kimberley, established in 1890 with the purpose of caring for the physical and spiritual wellbeing of local Aboriginal people. With the government, Beagle Bay became an institution implicated in the removal of 'part Aboriginal' children from their parents. The police had the responsibility of rounding up such children from around northwest towns and taking them to similar government institutions and missions (Choo 2001).

There is also legislation in the background of Martha's story. The Aborigines Act 1905 has special connotations even today because of its gross erosion of rights, resulting in forcible removal of children and internment of Aboriginal people onto bleak reserves, and into servitude and despair. The Act marked the start of a period of formidable surveillance and oppression of Aboriginal people. While the Native Administration Act 1936 consolidated the absolute rights of the state over Aboriginal people, the 1905 Act is symbolic of Indigenous oppression in this state. All states in Australia had similar legislation to supposedly care for, but primarily to control, Aboriginal people.

FINDING MARTHA'S STORY

My cousin Kathy and I were reading the Native Affairs files about the lives of our grandmother, Martha, and our great grandmother, Lillian. These two women had exciting lives and the records were thick with state surveillance and interference. We read how they were monitored, blocked and transformed at times into animals, always depicted as bad women of unsavoury characters, exclaiming, 'Poor Nan – poor old girls'. Because we knew the real people that the files misrepresented. We laughed at some of the things they were reported to have done: styling up and catching planes to and from Broome and Port Hedland – without permission, and not tolerating oppressive men. Our hearts were filled with joy at their audacity and defiance. The records tried to make them small and grubby, but we knew that their hearts and personalities were huge and bright and that they just wanted to be free women. Then we saw a 1943 report from the Commissioner of Native Affairs, Frank Bray, who wrote that Martha and Lillian were the original 'Mothers of Sin of the North'. We looked at this somberly and then we cheered, and lifted our coffees in a salute to our foremothers, acknowledging that their actions made us proud, their resistance was a joy, enacted in a time when resistance was dangerous, and that their resistance was for

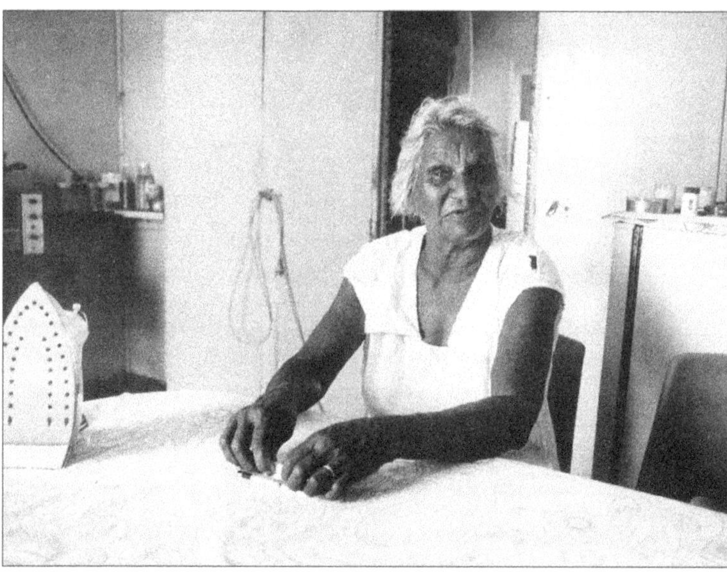

My grandmother, Martha Hughes. Courtesy Roger Garwood

personal freedom, not for any noble cause, but just to determine and to live their own lives without interference. May their spirits live on in us. (Dudgeon 2008, p. 1)

My grandmother Martha was an extraordinary woman. I grew up on the tales of her hard drinking and hard fighting and gambling. Apparently she could knock any man out with one punch. She presided like a queen over the Bamboo Lounge, the roughest bar in Darwin. I knew her later in her life, when she was sober, tall, handsome, straight-backed and fastidious in her personal hygiene, always well groomed and perfumed with talcum powder. She was charming and humorous when she wished. She was religious and respectable. However, one day when we teenage girls were at her place talking about boyfriends and romance, she paused from her card game of patience, saying, 'Hey, don't you girls worry! I have been around, too', and with supreme self-confidence patted her groin. Of course we upbraided her for being a rude old devil, but that is how we women talked together and, in any case, she smugly ignored us, flipping over her cards.

Yet, the memory of that confidence in her femaleness stayed with me. Despite the abuses, despite the assimilationist environments that imposed alien values and degraded us, in a time when nobody would have imagined the cultural renaissance that gives us pride in our culture, something unique survived in women like Martha – an appreciation of and pride in their gender and sexuality. In retrospect, in my grandmother I see two sides of Aboriginal women's self-perceptions of their sexuality: first, a quiet pride in their femaleness that does not subscribe to Western ideas of beauty or how women should behave; and, second, a history of their abuse and commodification during the process of colonisation.

My grandmother's story is one of many. The stories might come from and be about Aboriginal women in the Northern Territory or in Queensland as well as from the north of Western Australia since the broad brush of the story of Aboriginal women is the same across the country. Even though details of places, individuals and personalities might differ, the outlines of the stories of our foremothers remain consistent. A story other than my grandmother's that haunts me is that of Taralong, told by Hunt in *Spinifex and Hessian* (1986). Taralong was an older Aboriginal woman who worked as a shepherd on the Withnell's Hillside Station in 1891 in the Pilbara. One day she refused to care for the sheep, saying they could 'go to buggery'. She must have been hot and weary, tired of working for basic rations, probably in country that she once owned as a free woman. She was sitting under a tree when Withnell, the station owner, struck her hard with his bridle. She jumped up to retaliate, rushing at him with a stick yelling, 'Come on then, fight!' He picked up another big stick and beat her down. He beat her hard – long and severely. Taralong crawled off into the bush and died two days later. No charges were brought against Withnell. The only reason we know this story is because the case is in police records, a rare consequence to the killing of Aboriginal people at the time. The law said he had been provoked into the act and no charges were laid. Taralong's story illustrates that active resistance by Aboriginal women, as for Aboriginal men, was likely to end in beatings, imprisonment and death.

This is not an objective, distant story for me or other Aboriginal women who know it. I have carried Taralong's story for years. Her story, along with my grandmother's, resonates and cuts deeply into my heart.

BELLA'S STORY

Taralong could have been my great-great-grandmother, Bella, from Gija country near Turkey Creek in the Kimberley. The authorities forcibly took her child, Lillian, in 1909 to be assimilated and 'civilised'. I have thought about how it may have happened – did Bella run screaming and wailing after the party that took her 11-year-old daughter away? Was she stopped dead in her terror-filled flight to save her child and then beaten down into the red dust? Her sisters would have gathered around her, protecting, wailing and grieving. Did she grieve and beat her head with sharp stones as they did when a loved one died, the physical pain and blood an expression of the heart's anguish? The state and the church thought that Aboriginal women would quickly get over the removal of their children (Choo 2001), just as bitch dogs were thought to when their litters were taken. The tragedy of colonisation for Bella at a very personal level is that, as well as making Aboriginal people less than human, they also dehumanised and devalued her mother's love. Apparently Lillian's father was a white constable who had many Aboriginal 'wives'. He would have been the Native Protector of the area and by law have had the authority to remove 'half-caste' children into institutions, away from 'savage' influences. He may have sent Lillian away because he hoped she would have a better life.

Lillian was one of the first part-Aboriginal 'orphans' who was sent to Beagle Bay Mission as a result of regular expeditions to remove 'half white' children from their mothers from 1908 onwards. Lillian would have learned that her brown skin and grey eyes could have made her a favoured 'orphan', closer to white and, so, trainable. She would also have learned that being Aboriginal meant you were totally powerless. History is close for Aboriginal people: we daily live the consequences of decisions made long ago by the vast range of 'officials'.

MARTHA'S STORY

Lillian married William (Willie) Mungit, a Bardi man. It is family legend that William's mother, Jurud, found the famous Southern Cross pearl and traded it to white pearlers. Jurud lived in a branch shelter on the outskirts of the mission compound with other elderly tribal people. She saw her children taken into the mission culture, put into dormitories, Christianised and, in some sense, assimilated. She may not have been resentful of this, as the missionaries tolerated the local Aboriginal cultural ways and incorporated some practices into their own Christian rituals. The mission also provided food and protection.

Willie and Lillian became a model Aboriginal couple at Beagle Bay Mission. Willie worked as a casual labourer on the pearling luggers and together they had five children. Their daughter, Martha, was my grandmother. Willie must have been highly regarded by his white employers as he was part of a three-man crew who sailed the lugger *Enid* to Fremantle for refitting. Maritime records show that the *Enid* left Broome for Fremantle in late February 1928 and was never seen again. The crew was presumed to be lost at sea (Dickson 1994). The family lost their breadwinner and protector. Soon afterwards Lillian and her children, especially Martha, became visible in the Native Welfare records. In those records, they are translated and transformed into wicked, wild women, labelled and called 'prostitutes', 'sly as black snakes' and the 'Mothers of Sin of the North'.

I have served on the Parole Board of Western Australia for about five years. There I observed that the Native Welfare records can be likened to those of prisoners on parole, in that the level of control and surveillance in every aspect of their daily life is similar. Both are required to seek permission for trivial matters that free citizens take for granted: where you work, if you wish to move residence from town to town, who you marry, who you associate with and so on. If you breached conditions, you could end up going to jail. For most Aboriginal people living in Australia during that time, legislation made them parolees in their own country. How rigidly this was enforced may have varied somewhat from place to place but the overarching experience was similar. Unfortunately for Martha and Lillian, the Broome officials of that time were very zealous about imposing the policy to its full extent.

Martha and Lillian's crime was that they were Aboriginal women who wanted to live a free life. It is apparent from the records that the Native Protectors in Broome and other government authorities could not deal with such women. Concerns were expressed about their sexuality. Another one of Lillian's daughters was warned by the Deputy Chief Protector that her association with coloured men during the last lay-up season had been brought to his attention and that unless she mended her ways, 'I may find it necessary to issue a warrant for her removal from Broome' (DNA, File Note 349/30, Letter to Sgt Clements, Broome, 2 August 1934). Lillian had to obtain permission to remarry. And throughout, the records indicate that Lillian and Martha were considered to be of unsavoury character. They were 'proclaimed far and wide throughout the district as prostitutes' and the men they married were described as 'low types' (DNA, File Note 538/42, Letter to Sgt Tonkin, Port Hedland, 8 February 1944). They were watched and reported on; their movements were monitored. They tried to get exemption from the Aborigines Act 1905 and subsequent legislation – to get the conditional status of a free citizen – but were repeatedly denied because they were seen as women of easy virtue.

Martha became pregnant to a Chinese pearl diver, Ha Hong. The details of their private affair are put down in police records in a grubby, sordid manner. The Chief Protector of Aborigines requested that Ha Hong be prosecuted for unlawful cohabitation with an Aboriginal native half-caste. Martha refused to give evidence against him and the case was abandoned (DNA, File 159/43, Letter to Inspector Carroll, Broome, 26 October 1936). It must have taken some courage to stand against the authorities as she did.

She gave birth to my mother in 1936 and made ends meet by doing washing for families in Broome. Later on, under the title *Subject: Half Caste Women*, among other cases, the official reported that Martha was going with a Malay man: '[W]e will never stop her. I have spoken to her several times and the last time I spoke to her she told me she would have a man when she felt inclined and no one would stop her' (DNA, File 159/43, Report by AT Woodland, Broome, 1 March 1938). Coercive removal and relocation was a common theme in the files; it was often suggested that Martha's children should be removed from her and that she should be removed from town altogether.

The first two children of my grandmother, my mother Christine and my aunt Dotty (Dorothy Cox), grew up in Beagle Bay. Martha had to leave them there so she could work. The records state that Christine and Dotty were nearly sent away from their home country to Moore River Native Settlement, just north of Perth. When I first read of this planned removal from their country, my blood ran cold. My family history would have been so very different if this official whim had been carried out. Fortunately, for some reason not identified in the records, Christine and Dotty remained at Beagle Bay. For all its hardships, Beagle Bay Mission was not the hell of Moore River Native Settlement – a misery and a concentration camp, documented in Aboriginal autobiographies such as *Follow the Rabbit Proof Fence* by Doris Pilkington/Nugi Garimara and *When the Pelican Laughed* by Alice Nannup. My mother always said that at least they were in their own 'country' and had their mimmis (aunties) around them.

My mother, Christine Grimm. Courtesy the author.

My aunt Dotty (Dorothy Cox). Courtesy Dorothy Cox

In 1940 Martha and Lillian moved south to Port Hedland to find work and to escape the scrutiny of the Broome officials. They travelled back and forth to Broome, sometimes by plane, once even being interviewed by police who were not aware that there were warrants out for them. Martha and Lillian had broken the law by moving to Port Hedland without permission and warrants had been issued for their removal from Port Hedland.

Under the law Aboriginal people were required to obtain permission to marry. The records show that Martha was refused permission by the Commissioner of Native Affairs to marry one man, categorised as a half-caste. Later, she and another man (white), who she eventually married, wrote many letters requesting the Commissioner's consent. The authorities replied that they had no objection providing the couple lived in Broome.

Broome is north of the 20th parallel of south latitude – this was known as the 'leprosy line' and was legally designed to control the movements of Aboriginal people, as they were seen as responsible for spreading leprosy. Under the Act, every person identified as Aboriginal who wanted to travel south had to get permission to cross the boundary line. A letter from the Commissioner of Native Affairs outlined the concern in Martha's file:

> *The leprosy legislation was enacted by Parliament but in its wisdom was first of all investigated by a conference consisting of the Minister of Health, the Minister for the North-west, the Commissioner of Public Health, the Medical Inspector of Natives (Dr. A. P. Davis) and myself, and the main topic of the conference was in relation to the total suppression of the movement of native persons between Broome and Port Hedland.* (DNA, File 159/43, Letter by Commissioner of Native Affairs, 29 June 1944)

Martha and her husband-to-be lived in Port Hedland, south of this line. The authorities thought that Martha's future (white) husband might abandon the idea of marriage given conditions that would require him to relocate. The authorities saw this as a test of the man. However, Martha and her partner stayed in Port Hedland and married anyway, without permission. The Native Protector wrote that, despite Martha marrying a white man, she had still broken the law – she had crossed the line without permission. Martha wrote back defending her actions, stating her ignorance of the law, but to no avail. She and her husband subsequently were under constant surveillance, with authorities trying to catch her out drinking alcohol (prohibited to Aborigines under the Native Administration Act 1936):

> *Liquor may be found there but it would be hard to catch them drinking, and Martha is as cunning as a black snake. I have recently had to hunt this woman away from hanging about the town and hotel of a night, and she took it very bad. I do not know what can be done about this Martha, but she is a bad woman.* (DNA, File 159/43/129, part of a Report from CE Chipperfield, Police Constable 1912, Port Hedland, 15 July 1943)

The dossier on Martha states that the Port Hedland police noted she and her husband had left Port Hedland and were in Nullagine seeking work: 'She was defiant in her attitude to returning north and it was the opinion of the Police that she was deliberately flouting the law'. The records show amended warrants for Martha and Lillian's arrest as the authorities tracked them (DNA, File 349/30/144, 20 March 1944). Martha and Lillian returned to Broome to take Martha's children from Beagle Bay to live with them in Port Hedland. They were finally captured and detained in the Broome Hospital for breaching the leprosy line in the process of their travels (DNA, File 349/30/166, Report by Commissioner of Native Affairs, 1 June 1944).

WHAT TO DO WITH MARTHA AND LILLIAN?

Consideration was given to moving Martha and Lillian back to Port Hedland, but the Broome authorities saw their presence in Port Hedland as 'not desirable. They were seen as a menacing influence to the native situation south of the [leprosy] line' (DNA, File 349/30, Letter by Commissioner of Native Affairs, 29 June 1944). This entry in the records was made only four years before the great Pilbara strike, a general act of resistance and 'answering back' when Aboriginal station workers stopped work to protest against unequal wages and conditions between themselves and white station workers. Martha's presence and actions would have been discomforting to the authorities 'in control'.

Broome was not an option as the authorities were alarmed that Martha and Lillian might consort with the servicemen who went to Broome during the World War II. The authorities considered sending them to Moore River Native Settlement, but did not do so because there were 'sufficient troubles at Moore River without the presence of these 'hard bitten' women who [were] classed as prostitutes as well' (DNA, File 159/43, Letter by Commissioner of Native Affairs, 29 June 1944). Indeed, the authorities considered that 'there would be less danger to Broome if they [Martha and Lillian] were sent [to Beagle Bay] and kept there', though they worried that, because of their 'loose moral character', they would be bad influences in Beagle Bay (DNA, File 349/30/144, 20 March 1944).

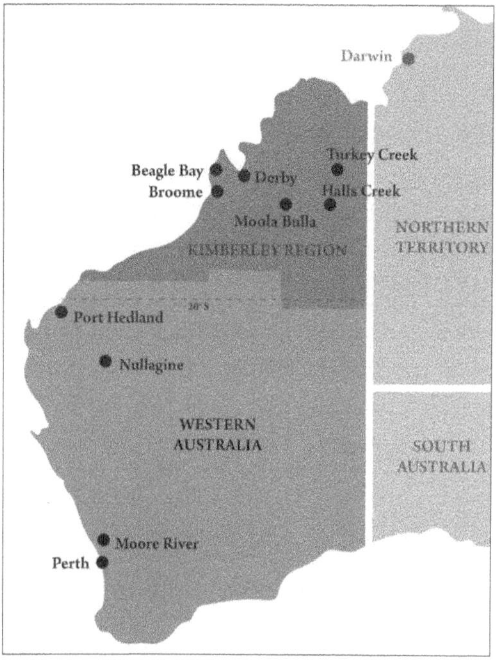

Tracking Martha and Lilian.
Courtesy the University of Western Australia

Eventually, removal to Moola Bulla Native Station (East Kimberley) was seen as the best solution – a long way inland from the West Kimberley coast. Moola Bulla was established by the government, in 1910, as a ration and cattle station to stop Aboriginal people from killing pastoralists' cattle and to encourage self-sufficiency by teaching them cattle-industry skills. It became a place to send Aboriginal petty criminals from all over the Kimberley. Orphaned children, many forcibly removed, were also sent there. The reason for Martha and Lillian's transfer to Moola Bulla is recorded in the file:

> *As there are many troops in Broome and in view of both native women's reputation for prostitution, and again as the Beagle Bay authorities do not wish them to be transferred to the Mission, I am faced with no alternative other than arrange for their removal to Moola Bulla Native Station for a period of detention. Possibly both women can be usefully employed at this institution. I regret being compelled to take such drastic action especially as both women are married to non-natives, but their recent unsatisfactory behaviour calls for firm handling of their respective cases.* (DNA, File 349/30/63, Report by the Commissioner Native Affairs, Broome, 30 May 1944)

Drastic action indeed. So, Martha and Lillian were, in effect, incarcerated for being 'wayward women' (Choo 2001). The Commissioner of Native Affairs made this clear in his correspondence:

> *Irrespective to whether or not these women received military permission to travel from Port Hedland to Broome, they also knew that they would not be permitted to return from Broome, as they have been previously warned to this effect. They decided to ignore the warning and now have committed to irrevocable residence North of the Leprosy Line. They are women of unsavory reputation and since they have always been headstrong and used to having their own way, it seems that they have deliberately defied the warning.* (DNA, File 159/43, Letter by Commissioner of Native Affairs, 29 June 1944)

The reluctance of the authorities to send Martha and Lillian to Moola Bulla is interesting. Moola Bulla, inland in Gija country north of Halls Creek, was like an open prison with nowhere to escape. The authorities knew that detaining the women at Moola Bulla would be a terrible experience for them. Both women saw themselves as mission women in contrast to traditionally oriented Aboriginal people, who were then regarded as uncivilised and were called myall or 'bush blacks'. Also, the women were saltwater people who were to be sent to the desert away from the family and people they knew. Lillian may have reconnected with her Gija family, but the women were effectively detained indefinitely in a foreign place. It would have been like being sent to an open prison under the Governor's pleasure – with no set time for release.

A Moola Bulla Station report of 1944 stated that the white husbands of both Martha and Lillian had objected in writing to their wives' detention, but to no avail. Martha and Lillian's letters of objection took on humbler tones with the passage of time (DNA, File 349/30/180. Report by Manager Moola Bulla Native Station, 5 December 1944). In 1945 their warrants were revoked as they were given favourable reports – they were 'behaving' and so subsequently were released. In 1947 both women successfully applied for a certificate of citizenship, which exempted them from the Act. From then on, records about them fade. They might have been more careful with the authorities or, alternatively, as citizens they may have escaped surveillance 'under the Act' or under more relaxed social times that followed the war. In any case, they continued to be hard drinking, fighting and free women, though the Martha I knew was a sober, respectable elder. She had given up drinking because she had diabetes. I asked my mother whether Nanna drank because she was oppressed and her spirit had been broken by her experiences in Moola Bulla, in periods of jail in Port Hedland and, later, Darwin. My mother replied that Nanna just loved her drink.

When I read *The Master Pearler's Daughter: Memories of my Broome Childhood* by Rosemary Hemphill (2004), I sadly contrasted the author's life with Martha's. Both women were born and grew up in the same small town of Broome in the Kimberley; one woman was from the affluent ruling white class and the other from the most despised group, the 'natives'. Hemphill was born white and privileged in 1922, only five years after Martha, but their lives were very different. Hemphill had the affluent whites at the centre of her story, Aboriginal and Asian people on the periphery. She read cultural diversity as a happy multiculturalism, implying equality and an absence of prejudice or inequality. Her Broome was exotic and uncivilised, yet she admitted that the geographical isolation made whites uneasy; her life was shored up with trips, usually travelling first class, to England and Perth. She seems to be a lovely person from her story and I don't resent her privilege, it just makes me sad for Martha. I resent that Martha was not regarded as human and worthy like Hemphill. Her life was empowered, she was valued as a human being. Riddett (1993) proposed that white women did not stay long in the frontier because of the harsh conditions there and Hemphill's story illustrates that even those whites who were born there did not stay. Hemphill eventually went to Perth and, later, to Sydney to live. Martha could not have left the north; she would not have chosen to. She lived for periods in different places but her country and kin were based in Broome and she was drawn back by that magnet. She spent her last years there and died when she was 72 years old. She had a long life.

CONCLUSION

Colonisation made some of our people powerless; it made them submissive, subservient and unobtrusive. Aboriginal people played humble in order to survive. I vividly remember how, when I was a young girl visiting at Beagle Bay Mission, the mob were playing cards (gambling) on a blanket under the trees and someone warned, 'Father coming, father coming!' That card game was packed up in a flash. Everyone smiled sweetly and obsequiously greeted the priest in honeyed tones. I was taken aback by the change of persona: the relaxed cheekiness, the community egalitarian feeling and pigeon English all suddenly replaced by the priest becoming the centre of everyone's attention, and everyone behaving with studied agreeableness and speaking a more 'proper' English.

I am sure that my grandmother Martha played the game of being humble, too, when necessary. Yet, the records show little humility and the woman I knew was not a humble person. Martha was an outstandingly assertive woman and to understand this, it is important to know that she was a 'mission girl' who had grown up in the mission dormitory system. Being a mission girl had great value in her place and time. She was trained in white ways: she was skilled at menial tasks, she was literate, she was of lighter skin and she had a fastidious personal hygiene that came from mission indoctrination. She knew that in the pecking order of racism she was not on the absolute bottom. Although the Native Welfare records vacillate and contradict themselves, naming her variously as an Aborigine, a half-caste or a native, Martha perceived herself as a 'coloured' woman, which must have impacted on her sense of self and given her greater personal agency.

Any discussions about Indigenous women needs to be placed within two overarching background contexts: the first is an understanding of Aboriginal history and culture prior to European contact, and the second is an understanding of the history of European colonisation in Australia. Without these two contextualising frameworks any discussion of Aboriginal issues would have limited meaning. Attempting to understand traditional Aboriginal culture gives meaning to the cultural values, behaviours and worldview of Aboriginal people that has persisted into and has been reconstructed into contemporary times. The other contextual framework, the history of European colonisation, is necessary because it has 'created' Aboriginal people as they are now and it is against this that we continue to define ourselves. From within these frameworks the topics of identity and roles of Aboriginal women can be discussed.

Speaking up and telling our stories ourselves is an important action in bringing back women's power and status. Over the last 20 years, strong Indigenous woman leadership has emerged across a range of locations in society to take up voice and position, not least in the academy. Indigenous academic Aileen Moreton-Robinson summarises the situation and way forward for Indigenous women:

> *Until recently history had been silent about Aboriginal people and has been told from a particular view. Over the last 20 years or so another history has emerged that tells both sides so to speak. Until very recently Aboriginal women have been invisible in this too. White Australia has come to 'know' the 'Indigenous woman' from the gaze of many, including the diaries of explorers, the photographs of philanthropists, the testimony of white state officials, the sexual bravado of white men and the ethnographies of anthropologists. In this textual landscape Indigenous women are objects who lack agency. The landscape is disrupted by the emergence of the life writings of Indigenous women whose subjectivities and experiences of colonial processes are evident in their texts.* (Moreton-Robinson 2000, p. 1)

While Moreton-Robinson challenges historical constructions, other Indigenous women scholars, such as Irene Watson (2007), are concerned with writing and speaking up women's authority, and the many other Indigenous women authors contributing to this text are telling their stories and truths. This augurs well for the future. A defining point in our journey in decolonisation has to be when Indigenous women and Indigenous men come together to discuss matters in respectful ways. I and other Aboriginal women were deeply touched by the Inteyerrkwe Statement, where hundreds of Indigenous men at a health summit in Central Australia issued a national apology to Aboriginal women. Here they acknowledged the hurt, pain and suffering caused by Aboriginal males, and acknowledged the need for the love and support of Aboriginal women to move forward. Capturing such respect and admitting our intent to do better in our gender roles and relations between Indigenous men and women will be a significant part of reconstructing identity and culture over the coming years.

BIBLIOGRAPHY

Atkinson, J (1990) 'Violence in Aboriginal Australia: Colonisation and its impact on gender', *Refactory Girl Newsletter*, 36, pp. 21–24.

Behrendt, L (2000) 'Consent in a (neo) colonial society: Aboriginal women as sexual and legal "other"', *Australian Feminist Studies*, vol. 15, no. 33, pp. 353–367.

Choo, C (2001) *Mission Girls: Aboriginal Women on Catholic Missions in the Kimberley, Western Australia, 1900–1930*, University of Western Australia Press, Nedlands.

Dickson, R (transcriber and compiler) (1994) *Ships Registered in Western Australia from 1856: their details, their owners and their fate*, Report no. 80/1–80/8, Shipwreck Databases, Western Australian Museum.

Dudgeon, P (2008) *Mothers of sin: Indigenous women's perceptions of their identity and sexuality/gender*, Doctorate Thesis, Murdoch University.

Edwards, H (1984) *Port of Pearls*, Hugh Edwards, Swanbourne.

Evans, R, Saunders, K, and Cronin, K (1993) *Race Relations in Colonial Australia,* University of Queensland Press, St Lucia.

Hemphill, R (2004) *The Master Pearler's Daughter: Memories of My Broome Childhood,* Macmillan, Sydney.

Huggins, R and Huggins, J (1994) *Auntie Rita*, Australian Institute of Aboriginal Studies, Canberra.

Hunt, SJ (1986) *Spinifex and Hessian: Women in North-West Australia, 1860–1900*, University of Western Australia Press, Nedlands.

Inteyerrkwe Statement (2008) Apology at the Aboriginal male health summit, *Australian Indigenous Health Bulletin*, viewed 1 March 2009, <http://healthbulletin.org.au/articles/apology-at-the-aboriginal-male-health-summit-2008/>.

Kimberley Language Resource Centre. (1996) *Moola Bulla: In the Shadow of the Mountain*, Magabala Books, Broome.

Lockwood, D (1980) [1962] *I, the Aboriginal,* Rigby Publishers, Adelaide.

McGrath, A (1987) *Born in the Cattle: Aborigines in Cattle Country.* Sydney: Allen & Unwin, Sydney.

Moreton-Robinson, A (2000) *Talkin' up to the White Woman: Indigenous Women and Feminism,* University of Queeensland Press, St Lucia.

Morgan, S (1987) *My Place,* Fremantle Arts Centre Press, Fremantle.

Nannup, A (with Marsh, L and Kinnane, S) (1992) *When the Pelican Laughed,* Fremantle Arts Press, Fremantle.

Pilkington, D (1996) *Follow the Rabbit Proof Fence*, University of Queensland Press, St Lucia.

Riddett, LA (1993) 'Watch the white women fade: Aboriginal and white women in the Northern Territory 1870–1940', *Hecate,* 19, pp. 73–92.

Smith, LT (1999) *Decolonizing Methodologies: Research and Indigenous Peoples*, Zed Books, London.

Watson, I (2007) 'Aboriginal women's laws and lives: how might we keep growing the law?', *Australian Feminist Law Journal,* vol. 26, pp. 95–197.

Wetherell, M, McGhee, P and Stevens, P (1998) 'Defining social psychology', in R Sapsford, A Still, M Wetherell, D Miell and R Steven (eds), *Theory and social psychology* (pp. 5–18), Sage Publications, London.

Wetherell, M (ed.) (1996) *Identities, Groups and Social Issues*, Sage Publications, London.

Primary sources

State Records Office of Western Australia, Department of Native Affairs (DNA), Personal Files

Personal files held at the State Records Office are closed to the general public and are available only to direct family members upon application. The following files relating to Martha were accessed as part of this chapter. A copy of each of the files is held by Pat Dudgeon, who is Martha's granddaughter.

WAS 2030, File numbers: 349/1930; 159/1943; 341/1947; 349/1934; 538/1944, 159/43/1944.

Legislation

Aborigines Act 1905 (No. 14 of 1905); *Native Administration Act 1905–1936* (No. 43 of 1936); *Native Administration Act Amendment Act 1941* (No. 4 of 1941); *Natives (Citizenship Rights) Act 1944* (No. 23 of 1944).

PROFESSOR IRENE WATSON belongs to the Tanganekald and Meintangk First Nations peoples of the Coorong and southeast South Australia. Irene graduated with a Bachelor of Law from the University of Adelaide and received the Bonython Law School prize for her doctoral thesis in 2000. She combines academic research with teaching and is a well-known activist for land rights and self-determination. She is a Professor of Law at the University of South Australia where, in 2016, she was appointed Pro Vice Chancellor for Aboriginal Leadership and Strategy and Unaipon Chair at the University.

STANDING OUR GROUND AND TELLING THE ONE TRUE STORY

Irene Watson

For me the telling of the truth – the 'one true story' – carries with it obligations to country and family and in the telling I understand that there is not one but many stories.[1] The term 'one true story' has been used across Aboriginal Australia and has different meanings according to the different contexts it is used in. In this context I am attempting to peel back the layers of various colonial understandings and constructs of 'Aboriginality', the 'Aboriginal problem' and the ever-demanded 'solutions'. In the telling of the one true story is the hope that we see through the colonial layers to enable a space in which Aboriginal voices can speak confidently, without fear of the colonial project capturing and containing our voices.

Obligations to tell the one true story are difficult and often seem impossible to accomplish living under the Australian colonial regime. Whenever we speak or write into this colonised space the question is always: what is it that we have spoken or written on and what gets left out or left behind? I also ask myself: what do you think you are doing when writing and recording First Nations experiences of life and colonialism, that which the

1 'Country and family' is used in the sense of relatedness or Aboriginal connections to place and peoples.

universities call research?[2] How true is my telling? In speaking and writing, it has been my aim to explore how to communicate the truth in a way that goes beyond the critical writing and interrogations that might change thinking and behaviour to, most importantly, acting upon that knowledge.

This chapter arises from work I began in 2005 in which I have explored the spaces that First Nations women's laws continue to occupy (despite an ongoing colonialism), and the tensions, contradictions and controversies which infect these spaces within the contemporary world. These infections arose from *terra nullius* – the colonialist idea that First Nations Peoples at the time of the invasion of Australia were without law, and this perceived absence of law was extended to Aboriginal women and our laws. The impact of *terra nullius* and the violence it brought to Aboriginal life has remained largely unexamined beyond its brief interrogations in the High Court decision in *Mabo*; however, the ongoing denial and refusal by the Australian state to 'recognise' Aboriginal women's law was the subject of and the conclusion reached by a Royal Commission inquiry into the alleged fabrication of Aboriginal women's law business.[3] The refusal to recognise the existence of Aboriginal law has impacted on Aboriginal lives and lands since the British invasion. The colonial violence responsible for the negation of our laws is rarely interrogated in contemporary discourses on violence and First Nations Peoples, but its impact and effect is reflected in the levels of violence which currently exist in First Nations lives. Colonialism is not examined as a cause of Aboriginal violence; instead the state has constructed Aboriginal culture as a core cause (Watson 2007a). This we have witnessed, as we have many times in the past, with the Northern Territory Intervention introduced in 2007 (Watson 2009).

---

2 The research space enables me to record the colonial project and its effects on our lives. In the past this space was dominated by research that enabled colonialism. In this space I am developing decolonising approaches aimed at recentring First Nations epistemologies.

3 The dispute over the existence of Aboriginal women's law was central to the Report of the Hindmarsh Island Bridge Royal Commission (1995). The Commissioner concluded that the claims made by Aboriginal women were fabricated and that there was no evidence of women's business to have existed in the Kumarangk–Goolwa Hindmarsh Island region. This went against the evidence of many First Nations Peoples who have supported the knowledge and understanding of Aboriginal women's business in the southeast region of South Australia.

In the development of my project *Law-full Women: An exploration of the self-determination of Aboriginal women's law, its colonisation and the possibility of the journey towards de-colonisation, to the place of the law-full woman*, I began to map the historical relationship between the violence of *terra nullius* and its impact on the lives of First Nations Peoples. I named this project *Law-full Women* to position my approach: that I view Aboriginal women as being and remaining full of law, our law. This land now called Australia was full of Aboriginal law prior to the invasion and, that notwithstanding, it remains full of Aboriginal laws. Our laws may not be visible to the non-Aboriginal, but they are laws which nevertheless reside in the land, minds, bodies and souls of First Nations Peoples across Australia.

The idea of Australia being full of Aboriginal law was rejected by *terra nullius* and it is still rejected by that same racist ideology today. The continent was claimed for a 'peaceful settlement' and deemed inhabited by 'native' peoples without laws. The recognition of Aboriginal law in the *Mabo* decision is limited to a context in property law and for the purpose of establishing a native title right. It depends on the existence of Aboriginal law prior to colonisation and its continuing existence post-colonisation. This right, however, remains open and vulnerable to the power of the colonial state to extinguish it. Yet, the greater understanding of our relationship to country is not acknowledged in domestic or international law. Law reform which considers the broader application of Aboriginal laws in domains such as caring and sharing for land and peoples, sustainability, surviving genocide and conflict resolution is yet to come.

In conversations with other First Nations women we have discussed the potential of Aboriginal-centred strategies to heal colonial traumas and contemporary violence. Many of these conversations have focused on the role of senior Aboriginal women, in particular mothers and grandmothers, as being core players in the futures of First Nations, as they were in the past. These strategies are not new and we acknowledged them as knowledges that existed before the invasion and colonisation, though the invaders never acknowledged them beyond paternalistic studies on the 'customs of the natives'. When the opportunity has arisen for First Nations Peoples to discuss our laws from our own perspectives, there are underlying common principles, such as the need for Aboriginal self-determination.

In reflecting on the impact of *terra nullius* on First Nations women's law, I have looked at how those laws have been ignored, but where retained, how they have been contaminated, interpreted, reinscribed and translated. I have previously examined Anglo-Australian governance models imposed on First Nations and concluded that those colonial models have consistently failed, throughout the colonial project.[4] This is to be compared with Aboriginal models which have worked well in building strong First Nations communities.[5] My experiences, observations and knowings have concluded that a decolonising approach works towards reinscribing the places of women's law, that is, as it always was, within the overall body of Aboriginal law. In naming this up I am not even attempting to identify what might be reinscribed, for this is a big process in itself. It is a First Nations process that will take time to recover and reclaim for First Nations futures.

TELLING STORIES – FOR WHAT PURPOSE?

In telling our stories many First Nations Peoples also carry the obligation to realise that story with its dreams and desires – whether they are for respect, kindness, sharing and caring – as through this realisation there is effective First Nations decolonisation and recentring of law-fullness. There is a need to go beyond simply the telling of stories, to journey on to a place where we are able to fulfil our obligations. I should also say here when referring to stories as 'law stories' I acknowledge that this is law – not simply story, but law.

When the British invaded our lands, the fulfilment of obligations became difficult to comply with and continues to be difficult. The impact of

---

4 The Aboriginal and Torres Strait Islander Commission (ATSIC) was seen as a model in Aboriginal self-determination, but it was imposed by the Australian federal government and institutional limits were set on the areas over which ATSIC had power and authority (see Watson 1996). The abolition of ATSIC by the Howard government did nothing to correct a failure to deliver effective Aboriginal governance models. Instead it devalued the position of Aboriginal Australia by leaving a vacuum on the question and possibility of Aboriginal representation. That vacuum is now occupied with Aboriginal individuals handpicked by the government whose views are closest to the political agenda of the state.

5 First Nations Peoples across Australia have established and run successful programs based on culture for the purpose of building strong communities and combating violence. Many of these programs were defunded during the decade of Howard's governance, but under the Labor government elected in 2007 and subsequent administrations there have been no moves to reinstate any of them.

colonialism is ongoing. In hardened colonised spaces, our stories concerning the consequences of greed and the need to uphold Aboriginal laws of conservation coupled with the sharing of resources to sustain the health and safety of First Nations Peoples now often fall on deaf ears. Colonising cultures read law stories that illustrate the obligations held by Aboriginal Peoples as myths and legends and commodify them, rather than use them to grow their awareness and knowledge of Aboriginal laws and ways of knowing the world. Yet, it is in these hardened spaces that we continue to breathe life into our stories and to enable the law-fullness that is intended with each telling.

In the past I have sat with grandmothers who have shared stories of being overwhelmed by the conditions in their communities, of being tired, of hearing children crying from hunger in their bodies and their souls. But we have also talked up positive solutions and strategies for building safe and healthy communities. The telling of stories is a part of the process of understanding, of naming up and affirming what is important to Aboriginal life. This is the work of telling our stories. However, occasionally the telling is done in a 'research space' which has First Nations Peoples as its subject. As a storyteller, a participant in the telling and sharing of stories, I have also become the 'subject' of the research process. But in my work I have taken a critical First Nations stand to interrogate the 'research' space, this space which has in the past ignored and failed to respond to the colonial traumas of First Nations Peoples so many times. I am committed to tell or to write truth informed by critical dialogue which takes us beyond the view of the colonial project that First Nations Peoples are objects. This journey compels us as researchers to act and transform the research project, so that the research focus provides the impetus for change, for decolonisation and a greater law-fullness. It is an ambitious approach, but to write for no purpose other than to communicate ideas is not enough – First Nations Peoples must realise ideas if we are to continue to stand law-fully in relation to our ruwi, our land.

I envision that complying with the obligation to tell the truth will amplify the marginal voices of First Nations. The discussions we Aboriginal women have invariably involve women standing strong. My story-song began a long time ago with my mother's grandmothers and it frames my thinking about the strength of First Nations women in our struggles to hold ground. This is an integral part of my worldview and consciousness. The conversations I have shared with other First Nations women have often centred on this question: what makes you strong and what keeps you standing in the face of a long colonial history of violence? It is my intention to weave those ideas, knowledges and conversations on the strengths of First Nations into a body of work that does not impose itself but informs our world. We talk up our strengths in the face of the colonialist constructs of native savagery and backwardness. The alternative to the deficit model or the dysfunction of Aboriginal Peoples and our communities is the choice of working towards a better empowered, decolonised Aboriginal space.

TRUTHFUL VOICES

In respect of the truth, Foucault (1990, pp. 38–39) asked the following question: 'I wish to know how the reflexivity of the subject and the discourse of truth are linked ... How can the subject tell the truth about itself?' From Foucault's analysis it would seem impossible for First Nations Peoples to tell our story truthfully. However, we are positioned, from a place that is without conflict or investment in the maintenance of the colonial project, to tell the truth(s) of dispossession, genocide and the struggle for our laws and their sovereignty. First Nations Peoples have less of a conflict of interest in the measuring of truth than those who inherit the colonial project and the desire to hold onto its privileges.

Historically, non-Aboriginal researchers and their institutions have mostly constructed First Nations Peoples as victims in research that is 'about us' and not emanating from our own lives. These research practices objectify us and have resulted in statements 'authorising views' of Aboriginal Peoples, describing (us), teaching about (us), settling (us) and ruling over (us) (Said 1978, p. 88); notwithstanding all this, this form of research practice is fairly open to questions of validity or the authenticity of its represented Aboriginal 'position' (see Watson 2007b on the problem of positing an Aboriginal viewpoint).

My reflections on the Law-full Aboriginal Woman have considered the politically marginal voices of First Nations women throughout the colonial project. Instead of focusing on the marginality of voice, however, I have focused on conversations which speak to our strengths and the strategies for decolonising First Nations communities, widening the lens to take in the vision of the autonomous law-full woman. The emphasis is on Aboriginal women's autonomy and the extent to which Australian law and Aboriginal law enable or dis-enable the autonomy of women, rather than interrogating the invisibility of First Nations women within the nation-state.

In previous work I have considered how different bodies of law speak or don't speak to each other, particularly on the question of First Nations women's law and autonomy (Watson 1998, p. 28). I have examined how the body of Aboriginal women is brought into Australian law and looked at what happens to Aboriginal law in that process of embodiment. Is Aboriginal law erased, as it is deemed to be by principles of extinguishment in native title jurisprudence (*Mabo v Queensland (No. 2)* at 15)? In this process of extinguishment, what happens to the body of Aboriginal law? Is it assimilated into the Australian state, without ground on which to stand or establish itself? What truths might be spoken in a space which is groundless and disconnected to the land? Why is this not named up as a species of genocide of law? Or by what other name might this annihilating process be called?

MAKING STORY A REAL ONE

While my work engages with critical questions that have been previously raised by postcolonial, feminist and race theorists, I along with others acknowledge conversations with First Nations women as constituting theoretical encounters (Dudgeon 2008, p. 16). In the past our conversations have been viewed by law and anthropology disciplines as 'natives telling stories', and they are about us telling our stories, but the stories should be characterised for what they also are: theoretical interventions. It is important in my view that these conversations are accorded this theoretical weight because they have potential to contribute more fully to decolonising strategies. It is Aboriginal-centric strategies and actions that are most relevant and compelling to First Nations futures.

The colonial research normative coming from the academic space would frame me as the 'objective' researcher. Research is never neutral, however, and in this project I, as a First Nations woman, am everpresent in each thought, discussion and analysis that is drawn. In addition, my presence and relationship to other Aboriginal women was essential to and reaffirmed the most important aspect of the work: the quality of relationships with the people we engage with. It is from these relationships based on obligations and reciprocity that planning strategies for our futures are most likely to be successful and produce positive results.

During the project I interviewed First Nations women and talked about their experiences and thoughts around the 'strengths of Aboriginal women', as opposed to them having to respond to an imposed research framework and its '20 questions' approach. It was the women's narratives, their stories and their reality that was told. We engaged in reciprocal conversations and thus I was inside the conversation as much as the 'participant', having the obligation to reciprocate and share my information and knowledge. It is a process familiar to First Nations Peoples; reciprocity is our law, essential to living law-fully. It is similar to ceremony, and in particular women's business, when First Nations women dance and one is invited to join; it is a moment of respect and reciprocity. One doesn't choose to dance or not to dance; respect calls one to participate as all others do and to move beyond being the passive observer or voyeur of the 'other' to being a part of the collective ceremony. So with the conversation or 'interview' we do not sit as an 'objective' observer; we make our contribution in a shared, reciprocal way. Yet, this is not the whole truth because the researcher has the power to continue, discontinue, edit and contextualise conversations, and the challenge for researchers is to continue to work towards dismantling the privilege and power mechanic they hold as the recorder of events.

The conversations between First Nations women are important because of their ability to open up a space in which we 'name our own reality'. As critical race theorist Richard Delgado has argued, reality is to some extent socially constructed, and telling one's story within an oppressed group can provide 'psychic self-preservation'. Delgado suggests that the dominant group tells stories in order to deny and minimise racism and that 'stories by people of color can catalyze the necessary cognitive conflict to jar dysconscious racism' (cited in Ladson-Billings and Tate 2006, p. 21). Perhaps a process of decolonisation begins when we place what has been the 'researched subject' at the centre of the inquiry, to decentre the power and the effects of colonialism (Bishop 2005, p. 110; see also Dudgeon 2008; Moreton-Robinson 1998). In my work I place strong women in the centre, taking up the comments of Mary Graham, that is, we have managed this entire continent for thousands of years and we carry that responsiblity to do so to this day.

Instead of using theory in a positivistic way, prioritising it at the expense of its study object, Foucault engages in a critical activity in which theory is derived from the analysis of the discursive production of, for example, prison life and thereby becomes practice. Theory does not express, translate or serve to apply practice: it is practice (Foucault 1990, p. 29). In the space of First Nations we were always self-determining, and we remain self-determining, even though the power of colonialism negates our authority. We will always carry the authority to be self-determining, for that is law. While I convened the interviews and initially set the boundaries, focusing on the strengths of women, the project has developed onward by dint of the collective conversations of First Nations women. I see myself as merely having opened up a space for conversation, to speak up the strengths and visions of First Nations women in our collectively held desire to rebuild strong First Nations. This project engaged participatory modes of research in which the participants have a reciprocal investment. While I have emphasised a positive focus and desire to rebuild strong communities, women have also been forthright in expressing the problematic of constructing the stereotype of strong Aboriginal women (from a conversation in 2006). So the need to acknowledge vulnerability, weakness, despair and women who may no longer have the capacity to stand up, let alone hold the ground, was critically expressed. In keeping the story real and true, these narratives have not been negated or overtaken by stories solely of strong women.

My work is an attempt to open up space for First Nations women to converse and continue to discuss and grow up strategies for positive futures. It began with the acknowledgement of the inherent right of First Nation Peoples to regain self-determination (Bishop 2005, pp. 114, 117–18, theorises self-determination practices as being an effective research strategy). So the conversations engaged with participants' ideas, on their terms. As the 'researcher' I was not positioned as the seeker of advice or the giver of voice to empower those 'other' voices, previously subjugated to mainstream state-controlled research. Here the intention is to subvert colonial practices, allowing space to speak or act outside 'normal' research frameworks, creating positive acts in the construction of decolonised spaces. Fanon (1968, p. 25–35) saw this movement towards decolonisation as setting 'out to change the order of the world' and the 'calling into question of the colonial situation'. Fanon incites us to question the power which is held by the colonial state as well as to look soberly at the work required to break up the colonial centre. An act of decentring occurs when the objects of research take on the speaking voice, to speak up their 'truth', the truth which calls for action (Fanon 1968, p. 25–35).

SAFE SPACES – THE JOURNEY TOWARDS DECOLONISING PATHWAYS

Australia's history and the continuing relationship between the colonial state and First Nations Peoples determines the research context. The researcher is often placed in the position of reproducing the colonial dynamic. The challenge is to create a decolonised space in which the subject of the colonial project can speak. How they then speak may remain the product of colonialism, so then the challenge is to create a space which enables the voice that speaks beyond subjugation to emerge.

Our capacity to provide a safe space in which to converse inside the colonial project is problematic. Historically, it has been a struggle to create these critical spaces for First Nations Peoples to speak; spaces to speak critically have not been easily available or accessible to First Nations Peoples.[6] We have only recently been able to access spaces to speak within universities, for example, or other centres where critical discourses are normally moderated, and these spaces may be disappearing. First Nations Peoples have instead taken to the street to protest or the parks to claim space for critical discourse. And while we go ahead anyway and claim those spaces to talk, I remain aware of the dangers for us when we do try to reclaim space to speak as sovereign peoples. The matter of sovereignty threatens the colonial state above all else, because when we speak as sovereign peoples we are no longer subjugated natives, and when we leave the space of subjugation we challenge the colonial authority over our lives. These spaces are similar to those which Fanon described as 'frontier spaces' and which

6 Across Australian colonial history there are many accounts of struggles for those critical spaces. The Aboriginal Tent Embassy in Canberra is perhaps the most well known, though there are many more spaces which were established before and following the Tent Embassy.

I have previously named as 'unsettled spaces' (Watson 2007c). Settled spaces are the assimilated, absorbed spaces of Aboriginal Australia, while unsettled spaces are the frontier spaces and those others – like the Aboriginal Tent Embassy in Canberra from when it was established in the 1970s onwards, Genocide Corner in Adelaide in 1999, Cockatoo Island and Victoria Park in Sydney during the 2000 Olympic Games, Camp Sovereignty in Kings Park, Victoria, during the 2006 Commonwealth Games and, more recently, Redfern Embassy – which flare up and provide First Nations Peoples with a voice to speak to Australia and internationally of our position as colonised peoples.

Challenges to the colonial project in the past were often met with the murder of 'natives' and some would argue that this still occurs today. Many more would agree that while the contemporary deaths of the native may not be caused by bullets, poisons and other physical violence, they are instead determined by poverty, homelessness, incarceration and poor health. Speaking the truth is hard and sometimes dangerous.

TRANSLATION: WHAT GETS LOST AND FOUND IN THE PROCESS?

My conversations inevitably began with and took their cue from other Aboriginal women, and in beginning a conversation in this way a direction on how to look or how to grow up any particular direction or development was not imposed. It was about starting the conversation from a position which respected the eldership of knowledges which still live in First Nations Peoples. From there, conversations flowed to visions of the future and the problems we as colonised peoples collectively confront. The project was a safe space for First Nations women to speak to each other about our ways of knowing this world without being pulled into the matrix of the dominant culture's frameworks. However, at the same time, our conversations risk commodification, appropriation and mistranslation as we battle to retain or, more accurately, decolonise a space and free it of those risks.

In this project conversations on culture and law were self-censored. Censorship of Aboriginal knowledge is difficult to explain to non-Aboriginal people who are often intrigued and want to be taken straight to the centre of Aboriginal law and cultural knowledge; I understand this as arising from the fascination with secret and 'exotic' knowledge. For example, telling the story of the Seven Sisters, which is about women's law, isn't simply the telling of a story but involves immersion into a process of law, life and being. The story is not fixed in time but relates to what has also touched our lives since the British invasion. There are layers of the story which are not told to the uninitiated, and in the same way there are layers of knowledge on law and culture of First Nations Peoples which remain private and unavailable for public consumption. Teaching outsiders or the uninitiated about Aboriginal law and culture is not simply a process akin to learning within the state's education system, where good grades, power, money and privilege can elevate levels of success. Aboriginal learning is based on different principles. The individual seeker of Aboriginal knowledge cannot just go to the story or the ceremony and have it translated and expect to then understand the law in the same way that they understand other narratives or stories or aspects of their learned education. This is because understanding requires more than an exchange of translated information. Which is another matter again: how does one translate across different worldviews? For example, the dominant Australian culture views land as a commodity, whereas Aboriginal people view land in relationship to ourselves, as we are to all things in the world we occupy.

When First Nations women come to speak about how we stand or fall on the land of our ancestors we occupy a contemporary space, but it is the same space in which our grandmothers had collectively sung the song/law of the Seven Sisters. We stand or fall in this same sung space, but now it is also layered by colonial traumas and laws. Here I don't want to engage in the process of interpretation or translation of the Seven Sisters other than to state: my knowing cannot be condemned by *terra nullius* or taken away by the fact of modernity or this contemporary context. This is because it is a song which sings and lives within my Aboriginal being, it sings to me who I am. I am not simply thinking about my identity as a First Nations woman, but about how I am able to stand on my grandmother's country and assert my law-full voice, which acknowledges the life of Aboriginal laws. I am not writing about the politics of identity and its performance throughout Australian legal history. I have been deemed many things, many identities, including barbarian, native, Aboriginal, British subject, Australian citizen, ethnic minority, Indigenous woman. I am proposing that the question 'who am I?' is framed beyond the battles of identity politics and who can speak and certify what about whom. I am thinking simply about how it is I can speak outside the marginalising politics of identity and know my song that sings in the land.

CONCLUSION

Aboriginal women's law remains strong in the minds and lives of many First Nations women. Our laws are layered across the country as they always have been, but the country now also carries colonial traumas and contemporary patterns of violence. So we spiral through these traumas inflicted on our Aboriginal places and spaces and law-full centres. We pass through time which is reaching towards eurocentric ideas of the 'end of history', which has 'progressed' towards this 'endpoint', but this model of progress is crumbling before our eyes, with the climate change crisis bringing a dim consciousness of reality to the Western idea or the non-Aboriginal idea of the end of history. But I also stand inside my Aboriginal women's law-full time and space, one which has always been, which knows that time is cyclical and beyond the notion of endings.

One of the aims of my work is to further elucidate the idea of women's law and the sovereignty of Aboriginal laws. In furthering this aim I work towards developing a decolonising text that reinscribes a women's law space, a space in which violence against women can be sorted and reordered, through the repositioning of Aboriginal women's laws. The critical question that this exploration raises is the possibility of such a place re-emerging, particularly where the imposition of the Australian legal system, which is meant to take up all the space, continues to question the very existence and sovereignty of Aboriginal laws.

ACKNOWLEDGEMENTS

This chapter was developed from the *Law-full Women* project, which was supported by the University of Sydney Sesqui postdoctoral research fellowship from 2005 to 2008. I would like to acknowledge Julie Stubbs for her support for the project and also Pat Dudgeon and Darlene Oxenham for their comments on this chapter.

BIBLIOGRAPHY

Bishop, R (2005) 'Freeing ourselves from neocolonial domination in research', in N Denzin and Y Lincoln (eds), *The Sage Handbook of Qualitative Research*, 3rd edn, Sage Publications Inc, Thousand Oaks.

Dudgeon, P (2008) 'Empowering research with Indigenous communities', *Ngoonjook: A Journal of Australian Indigenous Issues*, no. 32, pp. 8–26.

Fanon, F (1968) *The Wretched of the Earth*, Grove, New York.

Foucault, M (1990) *Politics, Philosophy, Culture: Interviews and Other Writings, 1977–1984*, Lawrence D. Kritzman (ed.), Routledge, New York.

Ladson-Billings, G and Tate, W (2006) 'Toward a critical race theory of education', in A Dixson and C Rousseau (eds), *Critical Race Theory in Education: All God's Children Got a Song*, CRC Press, New York.

Moreton-Robinson, A (1998) 'When the object speaks, a postcolonial encounter: anthropological representations and Aboriginal women's self-presentations', *Discourse: Studies in the Cultural Politics of Education*, vol. 19, no. 3, pp. 275–89.

Said, E (1978) *Orientalism*, Vintage Books, London.

Stevens, I (1995) *Report of the Hindmarsh Island Bridge Royal Commission*, Government Printer, Adelaide.

Watson, I (1996) 'Nungas in the nineties', in G Bird, G Martin and J Nielsen (eds), *Majah: Indigenous Peoples and the Law*, Federation Press, Sydney.

Watson, I (1998) 'The power of muldarbi and the road to its demise', *Australian Feminist Law Journal*, vol. 11, no. 1, pp. 28–45.

Watson, I (2007a) 'Aboriginal women's laws and lives: how might we keep growing the law?', *Australian Feminist Law Journal*, vol. 26, no. 1, pp. 95–107.

Watson, I (2007b) 'Aboriginal sovereignties: past, present and future (im)possibilities', in S Perera (ed.), *Our Patch: Enacting Australian Sovereignty Post-2001*, Network Books, Perth.

Watson, I (2007c) 'Settled and unsettled spaces: are we free to roam?', in A Moreton-Robinson (ed.), *Sovereign Subjects: Indigenous Sovereignty Matters*, Allen & Unwin, Sydney, pp. 15–32.

Watson, I (2009) 'In the Northern Territory intervention, what is saved or rescued and at what cost?', *Cultural Studies Review*, vol. 15, no. 2, pp. 45–60.

Watson, I (2015) *Aboriginal Peoples, Colonialism and International Law: Raw Law*, Routledge, Abingdon.

Cases

Mabo v Queensland (No. 2) (1992) 175 CLR 1

DR NERIDA BLAIR was born in the Kulin Nation, south central Victoria. She lives in Darkinjung Country on the Central Coast of New South Wales and works in Cammeraygal Country at the Australian Catholic University, North Sydney. Nerida has spent three decades working in universities in New South Wales and Victoria and over one decade in the public service in Canberra, Department of Education, Department of Foreign Affairs and with the Human Rights and Equal Opportunity Commission in Sydney. Education is her passion and she believes that it is the most powerful tool that Indigenous peoples have to fully engage in a safe and fulfilling lifestyle. Her current research interests include, Indigenous Knowings, ethics, white fragility and Indigenous leadership.

INDIGENOUS VOICES: IN THE CONTESTED SPACE OF INDIGENOUS AND WESTERN INTELLECTUAL TRADITIONS

Nerida Blair

Lately I have reflected a lot on why and how I speak and write and that is because I feel a pressure to perform. Why do I feel this pressure to perform, and in what context do I feel it? In this one. The pressure is to locate myself within a space where the muldarbi has been working for centuries in dismantling my Nunga being. The risk of entering this space is to become assimilated by the muldarbi, the challenge is to survive and remain a Nunga. In writing this article I see myself as being engaged in a process of translation, rather than one of co-option into the academic narrative.

I will write in a voice that is mine. A voice which may be construed by others as being a bit preachy, a bit angry, a bit sad, a bit desperate, entirely soulfully spiritual, dogmatically creationist. It is all of this and more, as I work towards a more 'perfect' place, a place that is still for me a long way off; that is the place where the grandmothers sit.[1] (Watson 1998, p. 28)

Like Watson and other Indigenous academics, I struggle with the correct voice to speak and to write in. I struggle with the correct space knowing that what I write – be it a doctoral dissertation, research articles and/or poems – is produced for the Western academy as much as I may want my voice and space to be for our communities. My voice, like Watson's, is that of a translator: operating from within a different worldview and translating elements of this into the Western academy. Where and how do I position my voice in what I see as a contested space between Indigenous and Western intellectual traditions? My voice is also that of a facilitator: a facilitator of my colleagues'[2] voices, colleagues who have engaged themselves in my research process. As translator and facilitator I choose to privilege my Indigenous worldview in all forms of writing.

This chapter presents my journey as an Indigenous academic drawing on multiple identities and finding a space for thinking and writing, a space that privileges Indigenous Knowings, not Western knowledge. This story is about trying to engage in 'intellectual self-determination': a space where I tested my linguistic competence; where country, spirit and soul became as much a part of my dialogue as rhizomatics,[3] action research strategies, postcolonial theory and so on. This chapter presents my struggle as an Indigenous person to decolonise my own journey. I do this without having the knowledge of my own traditional language. I do this by 're-creating' my own language and forms of linguistic competence. I do this not with the intent to create one voice, one story, but with the intent of growing a story, engaging in and

1 'Muldarbi' meaning demon spirit. 'Nunga' meaning a member of the Tanganekald People, custodians of the Coorong in South Australia (Watson 1998, p. 28).

2 'Colleagues' is the term I use to represent people I have done and will do research with. The traditional term would be research participants.

3 Rhizomatics refers to a paradigm of knowledge theory and research conceptualised by Deleuze and Guittari (1987, p. 7) which draws on the structures and components of rhizomes in nature. In the context of this work a waterlily and sweet potatoes are rhizomes.

interacting with the different voices and elements presented in this book, this story of ours as Indigenous peoples.[4]

WESTERN KNOWLEDGES AND INDIGENOUS KNOWINGS

As an Indigenous thinker and writer I seek and accept the space to coexist rather than to become a guardian of definitive truth as Western knowledge tradition dictates. This is fundamentally important in the appreciation and growth of our own intellectual traditions, our own 'Knowings', as Hokari identifies through Gurindji storying:

> *Maintaining the knowledge did not mean finding a 'right' story but widening the possibilities of stories. Information of different variations is preferred, pooled and maintained as a bundle of possibilities without judgement.* (Hokari 2000, pp. 8–9)

This exploration and bundling of possibilities is, as Watson notes in the quote at the start of this chapter, not a perfect place for our voices as Indigenous academics and in fact is 'still a long way off' being perfect. Yet we have a responsibility to reconceptualise the space and find our place through privileging our own epistemologies, ontologies, pedagogies: our Indigenous Knowings. As Indigenous academics rather than academics who happen to be Indigenous, is it not our responsibility to craft alternative thinking, positions and strategies so that we can find that balance Watson refers to?

Indigenous Knowings are unequivocally different to Western knowledge. Indigenous peoples from around the world have lived, created, developed and envisioned different models or patterns of Knowings which reflect the perspective that there can be no one definition of Indigenous Knowing:

> *We are not creating a grand theory or a universal conceptualization of Indigenous knowledge or heritage. We are intimately aware that each*

4 My book *Privileging Australian Indigenous Knowledge: Sweet Potatoes, Spiders, Waterlilys and Brick Walls* (Blair 2015) translates and facilitates my voice as well as a variety of Indigenous and non-Indigenous colleagues. The book has an accompanying webpage (http://spiderssweetpotatoesandwaterlilys.com/home/) which adds a different sense of time and space and presents non-linear storying. I encourage readers of this chapter to engage with the webpage to fully experience how I am positioning my voice in the contested space.

Indigenous regime is characteristic of the creative adaptation of a people to an ecological order. Given the ecological diversity, a corresponding diversity of Indigenous languages, knowledge, and heritages exists. For any research to seek to give a comprehensive definition of Indigenous knowledge and heritage in any language system would be a massive undertaking, which would probably be misleading. (Battiste and Youngblood Hendersen 2000, pp. 40–41)

Indigenous Knowings are quite often viewed by the academy as something less significant and inferior (Battiste 1996). In addressing this quandary, Indigenous scholars must face the challenge put forward by Battiste to rethink our use of the colonisers' language:

Linguistic competence is a requisite for research in Indigenous issues. Indigenous researchers cannot rely on colonial languages and thought to define our reality. If we continue to define our reality in the terms and constructs drawn from Eurocentric diffusionism, we continue the pillages of our own selves. (Battiste 1996, p. 232)

I do not wish to continue the 'pillage of our own selves' and I choose to use language that more accurately reflects our positions. This is often an awkward, uncomfortable position and path to take because as contemporary Indigenous scholars, we have often been institutionalised. We draw on our own experiences and our worldviews but often these views have been influenced by colonial interpretive monopoly, languages and discourses.

It is evident that there are strong and diverse articulations from Indigenous voices that privilege, to varying degrees, models and frameworks that nourish our spirits, our ecological connectedness and relatedness, our sense of belonging. There are commonalities across all the models; there is a form and sense that is localised, visual and organic. Some explore Indigenous Knowings, others Indigenous knowledge and others explore our position in Indigenous research. Underpinning each of the models discussed is pattern thinking, as described by Mowaljarli:

Pattern thinking is Aboriginal thinking. There is no big boss. Patterns are about belonging. Nothing is separate from anything else. This land is not separate from nature, people, the heavens, and ancient stories. Everything belongs in the pattern. There is no 'ownership' in pattern-thinking. Only Belonging. (Mowaljarli cited in Stockton 1995, pp. 42–43)

What is just as significant is that these voices also connect non-Indigenous, Western traditions of knowledge to a space that goes beyond 'othering', beyond hierarchy and systematisation of knowledge. We find enrichment.

POSITIONING SELF AS RESEARCHER

Part of the research process for my doctorate was a reflection of where and how I was positioned in the research. Other Indigenous scholars have explored the question of how we position ourselves in our research (Arbon 2008; Dudgeon 2008; Martin 2008; Moreton-Robinson 2003; Nakata 1998; Oxenham 2000; Rigney 1999, 2001; Watson 1998); it is common all over the world and is an emerging discourse on Indigenous methodology (Blair 2015). Positioning Indigenous voices as whole and privileging these was fundamental in my decolonising process.

My own journey crafts 'Lilyology' (Blair 2015) as a way to position my voice. My voice acknowledged kinship connections with and among each of my colleagues as well as with Countrys; in so doing it also acknowledged where the grandmothers and grandfathers sit. I was working towards a space where Indigenous worldviews could comfortably sit, centred and strong. I was constructing a model that was tangible and connected to Countrys, something that contributed to and enriched, that nourished the contested space between Indigenous Knowings and Western knowledge. Metaphor and imaging played an important part for me. I needed to find a way to express and communicate given that I do not speak my own Indigenous language. I played with words, their meanings and forms of notation.

In exploring text and notation I found that English words like 'country', 'story' and 'knowledge' didn't really convey what I meant. For example, 'Country' is so fundamentally different between Indigenous Knowings and Western knowledge. How to convey this? The term 'Countrys' embodies ecological systems that are so much a part of Indigenous Knowings: lands and waters, ecosystems of both and the world of the skies above us. It is not limited to geographical space and place as identified in Western knowledge. To convey this distinctness I chose to capitalise 'Country'. To give respect to our diversity as Indigenous peoples I pluralise the term to 'Countrys'. Similarly, I chose to refer to 'Storys/Storying' rather than stories because conceptually these are so different. Storying privileges Indigenous Knowings and is imbued with Indigenous context (Blair 2015, p. xv).

METAPHOR AND IMAGING

Mind mapping as a tool for Indigenous expression

Some years ago a friend suggested that I read a book about mind mapping called *The Mind Map Book* (Buzan 1997). As I read, that part of me that lay dormant was awakened, and the possibility of finding creative expression for my thoughts was triggered. I remember thinking, 'Why didn't I know about this before? This is the way I think.' I have heard this same thought expressed often in Indigenous communities throughout Australia over the years as they were introduced to this tool of expressing and articulating thought. I used mind mapping as a tool and process in developing material for a national education package for Indigenous peoples on human rights (Human Rights and Equal Opportunity Commission 1997). I am convinced that this tool provides a unique way to enable Indigenous peoples to communicate and express themselves.

Mind maps enable the idea of a nourishing core; one that expresses radiant thinking.[5] Mind maps are organic, rooted in a central idea; they embody rhythm, dimension, pattern, colour, metaphors and story. Mind maps facilitate non-linear thinking and focus on images and symbols as well as words if these are desired or appropriate. Mind maps were created with a belief that these would reflect more of the brain functioning as a holistic process – linear and non-linear. Mind mapping enabled me to connect through radiant thinking to images, rhythm and a sense of place. I drew parallels between mind map images and the many forms of Indigenous art. Indigenous art has a Story, has meaning and has a series of connected nodes, much like the root system of a bush or sweet potato as it grows in the ground.

While mind maps are a Eurocentric concept and tool, they embody significant elements that enable Indigenous thinking to be expressed. This allows people who have been victims of linear thinking education the freedom to express and reconstruct their own thinking and visions in their own ways. For me, and many Indigenous people I have worked with, trained and taught, mind maps can serve as a bridge that enables validation of our experiences of Indigenous Knowings. In a workshop on human rights

5 Radiant thinking is a process whereby thinking grows from a central idea and radiates out from this. It is opposite to linear and textual thinking, which is sequential and packaged.

I asked participants to draw their concept of human rights using colour, landscaping, images, symbols and words. With her permission, I used the story of a community leader (Alison Anderson) as expressed through a mind map in my book and on the web-page that accompanies the book. Her mind map is an illustration of the power of this tool in deconstructing oppressive social reality. In energetic discussions about decolonising our language and the whole 'human rights stuff", Alison went away and returned the following day with two new images (also seen in the webpage and book). As a traditional Indigenous artist, Alison found mind mapping to be a useful tool and that it served as a bridge between cultures. This was not the be all and end all, but a bridge that enabled satisfying expression. Alison employed these new ways of expression and used the images to express communities' thinking to the bureaucracy.

Another concept or way of thinking was revealed though this experience. Alison said, 'That mind mapping – that stuff is sweet potatoes'. For me this was a new way of perceiving; sweet potatoes were red bulbous things I might buy from the local fruit and vegetable market. After declaring me 'wamba' (a little bit silly and simple), Alison told me about sweet potatoes in her Country. She told how they grew, what they looked like and what they were used for. Other people in the training session joined in the discussion, talking in animated ways, yarning about sweet potatoes and yams and other bush potatoes in their own Countrys. Alison explained that a sweet potato has roots in and on top of the ground and it has a nourishing centre. Mind maps can also be perceived as a sweet potato growing in the ground (Blair 2015). Alison's final mind map looked like a spider's web, which led to one of those 'hold that thought, moments'. The spider's web emerged as a part of my decolonisation and imaging for my understanding and communication of Indigenous Knowings.

The sweet potato, the spider, the waterlily and the brick wall

The following poem is one of two abstracts in my doctorate. This poem was one means of representing my journey as an Indigenous scholar working within the academy and within my own communities. The poem has been modified and extended as my thinking has progressed (the original version is available in Blair 2008, pp. xxiii–xxxv). This illustrates a part of my own decolonisation process and was presented in the thesis as an alternative to the linear format that is required by the academy.

Waterlilys float listlessly; serenely atop fresh water
As the breeze blows.
Their leaves wide and flat hold fast on the water top;
A platform for the petals above,
The rhizomes below.
Rhizomes weaving their way further down in the darkness below.
Patterning,
Weaving, threading, connecting;
Reaching out to others, creating relationships, webs of connections
Petals delicate, elegant, vibrant, colourful
Varying sizes, shapes and shades
Curve and reach up to the sun, the light, the warmth
Smiling from the centre of the leaves,
Layering, overlapping petals
Joined by a stamen centred and strong,
Holding petals together.
The lily's core nourishes, feeds, sustains
A rich, creamy starch and carbohydrate,
Foundation for growing, for life, for living.

The colonisers came,
Constructed walls, fences, boundaries,
Walls of bricks.
Bricks made from earths substances; clay; sandstone and more
The walls cut off the source of water.
The flow of water is contained
Some lilys lay dormant,
Revitalised with each new rain,
Each new flow of water
Replenishing,
Nourishing,
Waiting for the walls to come down?
Searching for, finding mutual space to co-exist?

Spiders weave webs, woven webs.
Weaving fine, strong, transparent
Gossamer;

Sticky.
Vibrations felt from one end to the other.
Sensory, connecting, patterning.
Connecting across colliding trajectories,
Trajectories from Brick Walls, from waterlilys.

Sweet potatoes,
Rhizomes radiating out from a nourishing, rich core
A core of starch, of carbohydrate
Sustaining, energising, foundation for growing, for life, for living.
Rhizomes radiating above and below the earth
Inwards and outwards from the centre,
The periphery.
Sweet potatoes grounded,
Grounded in country
Grounded in Indigenous Knowings.
Sweet Potatoes
Patterning, connecting, radiating
Like
Spiders and
Waterlilys.

An important part of decolonising my own thought processes involved envisaging and imaging Western knowledge. I don't remember an 'aha' moment but I crafted the image of a brick wall to represent Western knowledge.[6] Western knowledge comprises many different disciplines within the academy, and the research paradigms and philosophies are embedded within the frames of both quantitative and qualitative research. Each discipline, each paradigm can be represented as a different brick. The bricks are made from clay (which comes from the earth) which can have different pigments added and blended to represent a form of interdisciplinarity or multidisciplinarity. The clay in my imaging of the brick wall is Western philosophy. The mortar holding the bricks of the wall together equates to Western knowledge. The brick maker is the academy.

6 The images presented here can be found in Blair (2015) and on the associated webpage: http://spiderssweetpotatoesandwaterlilys.com/home/

The bricklayers are the disciplines. The image of separate bricks embodies the concept of categorised knowledge disciplines. Some of the 'paradigm bricks' are coloured differently as they have embedded Indigenous perspectives in their research: bricks such as postcolonialism, critical race theory, anthropology, feminism, grounded theory, action research, cultural studies and phenomenology. Some of the 'strategy bricks' are tinted as they find greater use in fields engaging Indigenous research; these include bricks such as participant observation, oral history, focus groups and interviews.

As I reflected I noted that a brick wall has the capacity – in fact it is its purpose– to fence and to block things. It has the capacity to enforce boundaries. The saying 'I feel like I am hitting my head against a brick wall' emerged from my realm of thought because as an Indigenous person working in the academy I didn't feel that I was able to express myself and think differently, and I became frustrated, as I know our reality and expressions cannot be accommodated within the bricks of the wall.

Standing in relation to the brick wall is Indigenous knowledge, represented as a circle with a bush potato at the centre. Here knowledge is holistic and circular. It has a nourishing core that feeds Storys and Knowings and which radiates both inwards and outwards from the centre and the periphery. A Story is told. It is told again by another custodian who has the authority to add new information. The process continues. Western research philosophies such as hermeneutics tell stories, stories that build on stories, but they do this from a different epistemological centre – a Western centre or knowledge base. The research process we currently engage in centres Western philosophy, knowledge, paradigms and strategies. The researcher uses bricks from the wall as appropriate to build their centre, their research methodology. When doing research in Indigenous issues and/or with Indigenous peoples, researchers tend to look to the Indigenous knowledge circle and then extract parts of Knowings into the brick wall. These Knowings are translated and distorted and never return. The image presented does not centre Indigenous knowledges.

An alternative imaging centres and privileges Indigenous Knowings. Indigenous researchers can look to the brick wall and identify elements of the 'bricks' that may apply to our research journey. In doing this, we draw on the elements of the knowledge contained within the wall as we choose. It is at this point I change my concept from Indigenous knowledges to

Indigenous Knowings because it is imperative to make a clear distinction between the meanings embedded.

Indigenous Knowings became imaged for me as a Waterlily. The petals of the Waterlily flower are not homogenous. The petals, the stories, our experiences overlap and they have layers. The stamen holds all the petals together. The stamen regenerates life. The Waterlily has a strong, slender stem. It has wide, flat leaves that float on the top of the water. The stem and the leaves could be conceptualised as Indigenous Knowings. The Waterlily is a rhizome and with a rich, nourishing core. There are many different types of Waterlily, as there are many different Indigenous Knowings (Blair 2015).

CONCLUSION

There is a new language of research evolving where we as Indigenous peoples are actively positioning our voices, our Knowings. Within this there are commonalities and there are differences. Each person stands grounded in their own Knowing. We cannot grow Indigenous research without Indigenous Knowings. As Indigenous scholars, it is essential that we commence a process of knowing ourselves and our philosophies so that we come from grounded strong positions and are able to interact with Western knowledges in critical and discerning ways, and ultimately maintain our cultural integrity.

This journey and imaging has for me been an act of intellectual self-determination, one where I have been able to speak in a voice that posits survival and resistance. I have come to understand and respect this voice as different and not 'merely one co-opted into the academic narrative' (Watson 1998, p. 28). It is a voice still seeking the space for thinking and communicating ideas that emanate from a different worldview. Have I been able to 'maintain harmony and balance in being me' (Watson 1998, p. 28) while engaging in a communication of my ideas within the academy? This has been a starting point for me. For you the reader, the author, the thinker, how do you position your voice, yourself, in the contested space, the space in between Indigenous and non-Indigenous intellectual traditions?

BIBLIOGRAPHY

Arbon, V (2008) *Arlathirnda Ngurkarnda Ityirnda. Being-Knowing-Doing: De-Colonising Indigenous Tertiary Education*, Post Pressed, Teneriffe, Queensland.

Battiste, M (1996) 'Indigenous knowledge and research: enabling the autumn seed', in *Contemporary Issues in Aboriginal and Torres Strait Islander Studies,* Jumbunna CAISER, University of Technology, Sydney.

Battiste, M and Youngblood Henderson, J (2000) *Protecting Indigenous Knowledge and Heritage: A Global Challenge* (2nd edn), Purich Publishing, Saskatoon, Canada.

Blair, N (2008) 'Sweet potatoes, spiders and waterlilys: privileging Australian Indigenous knowledges. Epistemological consequences of knowledge production', unpublished thesis, University of Newcastle.

Blair, N (2015) *Privileging Australian Indigenous Knowledge: Sweet Potatoes, Spiders, Waterlilys and Brick Walls*, Common Ground Publishing, Champaign, Illinois.

Buzan, T (1997) *The Mind Map Book,* BBC Books, London.

Deleuze, G and Guattari, F (1987) *A Thousand Plateaus: Capitalism and Schizophrenia,* trans. B Massumi, University of Minnesota Press, Minneapolis.

Dudgeon, P (2008) 'Empowering research with indigenous communities', *Ngoonjook: A Journal of Australian Indigenous Issues*, no. 32, pp. 8–26.

Hokari, M (2000) 'History happening in/between body and place: journey to the aboriginal way of historical practice', in *Proceedings of the Habitus 2000 Conference*, Curtin University of Technology, Perth.

Martin, K (2008) *Please Knock Before You Enter: Aboriginal Regulation of Outsiders and the Implications for Researchers*, Post Pressed, Teneriffe, Queensland.

Moreton-Robinson, A (2003) 'Introduction: Resistance, recovery and revitalisation', in M Grossman (ed.), *Blacklines: Contemporary Critical Writings by Indigenous Australians*, Melbourne University Press, Melbourne, pp. 127–31.

Nakata, M (1998) 'Anthropological texts and Indigenous standpoints', *Australian Aboriginal Studies,* no. 2, pp. 3–12.

Oxenham, D (2000) *'Aboriginal Terms of Reference': The Concept at the Centre for Aboriginal Studies,* Discussion Paper 27, Curtin Indigenous Research Centre, Perth.

Rigney, LI (1999) 'Internationalisation of an Indigenous anticolonial cultural critique of research methodologies', *Wicazo Sa Review*, vol. 3, pp. 109–21.

Rigney, LI (2001) 'A first perspective to Indigenous Australian participation in science: framing Indigenous research towards Indigenous Australian intellectual sovereignty', *Kaurna Higher Education Journal,* vol. 7, pp. 1–13.

Stockton, E (1995) *The Aboriginal Gift: Spirituality for a Nation,* Millenium Books, Alexandria, New South Wales.

Watson, I (1998) 'Power of the muldarbi, the road to its demise', *Australian Feminist Law Journal*, vol. 11, pp. 28–45.

DR SANDY O'SULLIVAN is a Wiradjuri Aboriginal woman (central New South Wales). She is an academic and Director of the Centre for Collaborative First Nations' Research at Batchelor Institute of Indigenous Tertiary Education in the Northern Territory. She holds a PhD in Fine Art and Performance, in which she focused on the intersections of sexuality, gender and Indigeneity. For more than 20 years she has taught and researched across performance, design and First Nations identity. Sandy is an enduring Australian Learning and Teaching Fellow and has recently completed an internationally focused Australian Research Council program, examining the representation and engagement of First Peoples across 450 museums.

HOW TO (NOT) DEFINE ABORIGINAL LESBIAN IDENTITY

Sandy O'Sullivan

The identity issues of Aboriginal women is an increasingly important area of writing and reflection with a wealth of material exploring our struggle for equality, participation and engagement. In particular, the work developed by the contributors to this book has played a significant role in creating a framework of understanding and in relating the depth of our representations. In counterpoint to the richness of material on the broader gender struggle in Aboriginal women's lives is a dearth of discourse on the experience of Aboriginal lesbians. In this chapter I explore some of the questions that underpin lesbian identity issues in the contemporary Aboriginal experience and posit a rationale for why a straightforward historical review may not deliver the same benefits as it has for the discussions around gender representation.

When Destiny Attenborough, a mockumentary character portrayed by Aboriginal comedian Trisha Morton-Thomas, broadcast an ethnography of lesbian culture in Alice Springs (Dare 2007), she did so without the cushioning of a range of existing ethnographic material. When Lou Bennett spoke in an autobiographical performance about the strength required to leave a community that she saw as unsafe for her dual identities as Aboriginal and lesbian, she spoke to a wide audience of viewers who may have otherwise not heard her story (Roberts 2007). When Deborah Cheetham used the vehicle of *White Baptist Abba Fan* to speak of the difficulty of accounting for the influence of religion, culture, removal and sexuality, she struck a chord in the cultural space of being an Aboriginal woman facing these same challenges and dealing with the complex circumstances of these disconnections (Cheetham 2001). These untethered yet important moments create a space for questions around sexuality and its impact on identity; this chapter explores and challenges whether these contributions create a landscape of understanding of the Aboriginal lesbian experience. These works, delivered through the public domains of popular entertainment, provide moments to their audience that have no broader responsibility to educate and inform, nor to represent a single unified note on the First Nations lesbian experience. Yet these moments are significant in creating sites of recognition around how sexuality and Indigeneity may converge; in describing the specific experience of being a First Nations woman and a lesbian; and in creating in this difficult intersection an opportunity to ponder whether the experience as Aboriginal lesbians is so different to that of our straight sisters.

In 2007, the United Nations Permanent Forum on Indigenous Issues distributed a fact sheet that proposed a series of defining characteristics of Indigenous peoples. These identifiers or markers are intended, according to the fact sheet, to contribute to a 'modern understanding' of the distinct profile of Indigenous peoples:

- self-identification as indigenous peoples at the individual level and accepted by the community as their member
- historical continuity with pre-colonial and/or pre-settler societies
- strong link to territories and surrounding natural resources
- distinct social, economic or political systems
- distinct language, culture and beliefs
- form non-dominant groups of society
- resolve to maintain and reproduce their ancestral environments and systems as distinctive peoples and communities (United Nations 2007, p. 1).

As an Aboriginal woman who has emerged from the cultural space of dispossession, generational poverty, incessant attempts at language removal and the genetic interjection of colonisation, it is difficult to accept the application of a fact sheet that suggests 'historical continuity' or 'distinct language', let alone read the other markers as anything other than marking us according to our marginalisation.

Many of the concerns in proposing these indicators of Indigeneity reflect the impossibility of marking out a pan-Indigenous experience that encapsulates the diversity of First Nations Peoples. This same difficulty arises in discussing the experience of Aboriginal women in a way that reflects our diversity and difference alongside our shared experiences. We tell our stories one by one because our experiences are multifarious and variously influenced. While there may be convergence and some similarities, our diverging individual experiences disrupt a convenient forming pattern and are often a disconnected result of the intentional processes of dispossession – we are diverse. Against this backdrop, any attempt to create a space to discuss a singular representation of what it is to be 'lesbian' is as problematic as it is to define 'Indigenous' itself. Indeed, the use of 'First Nations' to define our multiple ethno-cultural identities has only recently become broadly accepted, with the recognition of the plurality inherent in 'nations'. Writing a unified or easily gendered or racialised identity is not only problematic, but also risks further containment and marginalisation in being identified into a yet smaller group around sexuality. Perhaps, then, the moments retold by Morton-Thomas, Bennett and Cheetham have greater currency because they acknowledge how the individual, reflexive approach can create a space of discussion and an opportunity to rediscover our true interconnectedness as Aboriginal women. It is their diverse experience and their individual engagement that shows our resilience as First Nations women.

If comparative analysis or historical review does not yield a unified understanding of Aboriginal lesbian identity through representation, a common link emerges to the moments explored in the broader Aboriginal autobiographic and recent ethnographic record of identity, belonging, rejection, isolation and resolution. What are the broader, direct questions posed to an Aboriginal lesbian? Does the identification of being a lesbian add a different dimension to our landscape of belonging and, if so, how? Is it possible that Aboriginal lesbians require a greater level of acceptance in our own communities? Are we shunned in our Indigenous communities? Are we accepted in our communities? Does our sexuality matter? Does it vary from Indigenous community to Indigenous community? A serious body of work has not yet been completed that poses any of these questions and, perhaps for some of the reasons touched on here, it would be difficult to argue conclusively that Aboriginal lesbians are more or less likely to be treated differently within our own cultural communities. Such a study could also prove difficult because, by drawing distinct identity markers, we are applying the lens of the coloniser to draw distinctions across gender, sexuality, behaviour roles. As Bundjalung scholar Maddee Clark suggests, gender and sexuality across the ethnographic record have been controlled and defined by the coloniser (Clark 2014).

In Martin Flanagan's 'Is reconciliation dead? Or will white Australia finally listen?', an article written for *The Age* in 2006, he recounts two 'stories' intended to demonstrate a confusion over the paths to reconciliation between White and Indigenous Australia. These conflated stories reveal his confusion about transgendered Aboriginal women attending a public event and seemingly being accepted by their community in light of a conversation he had had years before:

> *Some years ago, an old traditional woman from northern Australia stayed with me. I asked what happened to homosexual youths in her tribe in 'the old days'. She said they were taken out and killed. Therefore, to the question – what was the place of homosexuals in traditional Aboriginal culture? – I can merely offer those two stories from different parts of Australia plus a few snippets gathered elsewhere.* (Flanagan 2006)

He confuses sexuality with gender by remembering an exchange about homosexuality while being motivated by another remembering that clearly focuses on gender. In doing so he proposes a dangerous misrepresentation of these highly selective anecdotal moments as evidence of a conflicting voice in the Indigenous experience. Who was this woman who was asked the question; what was her role in her community? Did she understand that her comments would be repeated years later to summarise an Indigenous position on homosexuality pre-colonisation? Most importantly, how would she have responded if the question had actually been about gender and not about sexuality? These questions are pertinent because Flanagan purported to promote the value of listening to First Nations voices delivering the truth of our experiences over listening to interpretations by others, though ironically no queer Aboriginal person had a voice in this article. And so, in the context of two disparate moments in the life of the interviewer, he has sought to create a conclusion that defines for his readership – a readership that he assumes is unknowing of an authentic Aboriginal understanding – a sense that homosexuality is managed quite differently in Aboriginal culture than it is in the broader population.

Colouring the Rainbow: Blak Queer and Trans Perspectives – Life Stories and Essays by First Nations' People of Australia aims to provide some further clarification on these problematic and fractured views of, and sometimes within, our communities (Hodge 2015). A collection of stories and essays from Aboriginal and Torres Strait Islander Peoples who identify as queer, it uses the real voices of First Nations Peoples to challenge these messy assertions about a lack of flexibility in our communities, both in a historic and contemporary context. The book and its component chapters builds on the seminal work, *Peopling the Empty Mirror: The Prospects for Lesbian and Gay Aboriginal History* (Dunn/Holland et al. 1994), a collaborative essay by First Nations and non-Indigenous scholars that challenged the conflated fantasy of culture promoted by commentators such as Flanagan through the representation of the real lives of First Nations Peoples across Australia. In Maddee Clark's response essay, she updates the context of the earlier text by providing an Aboriginal lesbian lens that is inclusive, but not reductive, and by exploring perceptions that not only frame us as disadvantaged, but also diminish our diversity (Clark 2015, p. 251). Others take on both First Nations Peoples and spurious non-Indigenous scholars who have claimed we are outliers to the central community (Baylis 2015, p. 3; Goudie 2015, p. 130; Monaghan 2015, p. 195). An overarching theme of *Colouring the Rainbow* is the invocation of diversity within our sexuality community and an avoidance of singular tropes of representation across both sexuality and Indigeneity.

There is some material that purports to show evidence of how homosexuality in traditional Indigenous Australian groups was historically acknowledged, but this documented 'evidence' is not included here as the process of gathering ethnographic material has itself come under scrutiny in recent years. *Colouring the Rainbow* gives a more comprehensive treatment of the ethnographic record which challenges the reductive perspective on sexuality such research into our communities has reflected. At the risk of conflating the same gender and sexuality identifiers as Flanagan does, a significant challenge to the early anthropological studies of the Tiwi Islands has come from the Tiwi Sistergirls, a group of transgendered women, who have indicated that it was the anthropologists' failure to understand that their culture simply was different to the dominant White culture and could not neatly fit within their frame of reference, that removed mention of the Sistergirls from the anthropological record (Yunkaporta 2006). Where we are now finding ways to speak our own truths through performance, writing and other acts of public engagement, this erasure from our histories will continue to be challenged.

Aileen Moreton-Robinson's central theme in *Talkin' Up to the White Woman: Indigenous Women and Feminism* (2000) – a text that has proven seminal in proposing a complex understanding of who we are as Aboriginal women – suggests that we do not play a tidily Indigenised version of otherwise feminist roles, and that our complex agency does not require this alignment. Moreton-Robinson's assertions therefore provide a basis for challenging the convenient cultural shift from straight Aboriginal woman to Aboriginal lesbian; our identities – like our experiences – are complex and diverse, and are not Black versions of the negotiated experience of White lesbians. Similarly, if the interest in reasserting from outside the idea that our communities will not accept us, but our sexuality communities will, is around the individual experience of rejection that is deeply felt and tragic, it forgets that this also occurs across the White experience.

This will, of course, also challenge some of our own people's perspectives on sexuality. Invoking bell hooks's challenge to the manufactured culture that created a homophobic subtext across her own African American community, there is a resonance in her description of how communities become exclusive and resistant to diversity within. In 'Homophobia in Black Communities', she proposes that it is more about poverty than about culture and that poverty encourages exclusivity and coherence, thereby punishing diversity (hooks, 1989, pp. 120–21). The inability to turn back the clock of oppression, introduced and imposed religion and cultural dominance, and the wide-ranging fallout of colonisation would indicate that any current survey of attitudes to a lesbian cohort across the Aboriginal community may deliver a confusing and inconsistent result. The context is illustrated in Ruben Bolling's satirical cartoon that suggests the IQ testing of African Americans would improve against the White population if White people were forced into removal from their own country, slavery and oppression of language and culture, with the accompanying health, education and social disadvantages (Bolling 2007).

This diversity is played out by Morton-Thomas and writer/director Sonja Dare in *Destiny in Alice,* which deploys group and individual interviews with Aboriginal and non-Aboriginal participants about their experiences of being a part of the lesbian community of Alice Springs. The high Aboriginal population of the town frames the questions around Aboriginality as a key issue and delivers a moment of insight that explores identity. When Morton-Thomas, in character as Destiny Attenborough, poses the question of acceptance of lesbian identity in their home communities, the Aboriginal participants provide a different kind of answer in their group interview than they do in the one-on-one exchange. Significantly, in the group response, one interviewee discusses general attitudes rather than specific moments of acceptance, suggesting a resilience and that support for diversity is inherent in Indigenous communities. In the individual interview, the same participant is more introspective and they are no longer asked, or perhaps required, to defend the responses of their community, but to speak to their own, more complex, actual history. The humour of the mockumentary and the willingness of the participants to tell their stories makes it no less compelling as an insight into the patterns and moments in the lives of Aboriginal lesbians. It does, however, as with the other popular culture renditions of identity mentioned earlier, provide a space for anecdote that does not require the formal, rigorous academic rhetoric that may, if the argument of the problematic data-gathering holds, be no more valid or relevant, because it focuses on the individual experience in all its complexity.

So what responsibility, if any, do we have as Aboriginal lesbians to promote and discuss our sexual identity? I have frequently heard from fellow academics that my work on gender and sexuality has no intrinsic Indigenous resonances for them. As an academic who has largely taught in mainstream areas, I have found this both challenging in terms of my identity and a relief in light of constantly having to manage a response and provide pathways of understanding in a way that others might comprehend and accept as Aboriginal. The answer, as always, is that I find it impossible to extricate being Aboriginal from any discussion on identity, as it is my central cultural identity.

In counterpoint to this observation, some years ago I attended several

Indigenous researcher forums. At a time when there were few discipline-based, First Nations-controlled conferences, these forums provided a national platform to support early-career Aboriginal and Torres Strait Islander researchers in discussing and disseminating the findings of their varied work. At these forums, I have had an opportunity to explore whatever my field was; at the time I was undertaking studies across gender and sexuality and the focus of this research may have been seen as seemingly disconnected from my experience as an Aboriginal woman. At two of these conferences I gave papers, neither of which had a clear connection to First Nations Studies, but rather drew on the idea that the conference was for Indigenous researchers to gain feedback on their work, regardless of the connection to Indigenous matters. The data I was using focused on Drag King – the female performing as male, the inverse of Drag Queen – and the informal 'performance' within lesbian culture. With none of the data clearly focused on Aboriginal women, I had understood why researchers at the non-Indigenous conferences pondered why I talked about Aboriginality at all, but at these Indigenous forums that focused on our complex lives, identities and work, I was encouraged by the broader community of practice – my First Nations colleagues – to focus on the research itself both within and outside the context of my Aboriginality. This experience allowed my research to grow by inhabiting Dudgeon and Fielder's (2006) invocation of Bhabha's idea of the 'third space', by promoting interaction and merging the creative and meaningful moments of confluence, where the work became more than its composite parts outside the boundaries of the standard academic structure.

This freedom from potential ghettoisation and siloing of our work is key to understanding that there are other factors that affect our identity beyond the external view of our Aboriginality, and that in order for us to be recognised beyond tidy identity markers we must assert our rights to inhabit these spaces. We must continue to challenge the expectations of our broader communities, at the same time as recognising that identity markers can be used to create avenues of strength that may otherwise be seen as deficit.

Perhaps this challenge to a tidy explanation of identity is best demonstrated in *White Baptist Abba Fan*, an autobiographical performance by acclaimed opera performer Deborah Cheetham. Her moment of crisis and loss of identity occurs when members of her church cannot reconcile her religion with her coming out as a lesbian and so they shun her. She goes on to find community in the space of her sexuality. Throughout this is the underpinning reality of her experience as a child taken under the racist practices that are now framed as Stolen Generations (HREOC 1997). Cheetham (2001) states that her 'journey has always been to find the path from White Baptist Abba Fan to the gay Koori opera singer', suggesting that sexuality and Indigeneity are not the only defining characteristics that we inhabit as individuals, but that our diversity itself can change and adapt, and that a containing identity label placed on us will not reflect that diverse ideology and experience.

A key to further exploring how lesbian identity does not exist in opposition to our identity as Aboriginal women is to recognise that we share many of the same struggles with our heterosexual sisters. When Schiwy talks of the expectations of heteronormativity in highly politicised street performance enacted by Indigenous women in Bolivia, she describes a moment of transgression demonstrated through a performed lesbian interaction. The entire performance/action is framed as 'not only a critique of global power relations but also of internal colonialism where racism fractures the concept of gender' (Schiwy 2007, p. 271). This moment exposes heteronormativity as an absurd addendum to an otherwise consistent message that diversity exists, in part though a performance that challenges the notion that Indigeneity trumps lesbianism, or that any marker trumps any other, in the identity stakes.

This recognition that our identities as Aboriginal women and as Aboriginal lesbians, while interconnected, cannot be easily isolated or merged is evident in a range of research used to determine, and sometimes guide, our destinies. The blending of multiple category identifiers is often ignored by researchers who may otherwise wish to focus on the convergent factors in our broad community as a much studied group. This is a risk realised in the heavily cited 'The epidemiology of suicide and attempted suicide among young Australians', which has significant data and analysis of both Aboriginal youth suicide and suicide among young lesbians (Cantor and Neulinger 2000). There is no moment, perhaps no opportunity, within this report for a merging of these two sets of metadata, particularly where it would significantly reduce the strength of the data by reducing the sample size. This is yet another set of data unavailable to us, one that crucially could – using extrapolated and emerging evidence gathered here and internationally – demonstrate a crisis in our lived experiences that could be addressed or averted. Again, there is work beginning on this. Aboriginal and Torres Strait Islander man Dameyon Bonson's Black Rainbow has cited these emerging international studies, and called for a greater review of the lived experience across our diverse communities in order to provide understanding and support, and to avert what could be a national tragedy in youth suicide among Aboriginal queer communities (Bonson 2016).

There are also strategies to assert a layer of diversity and insinuate our experience through own authorship. *The Vagina Monologues* (Ensler 2001) is an American performance work that is frequently reproduced in many parts of the world. It focuses on retold moments from the lives of women from a range of communities and asserts a women-positive approach. The text has been heavily critiqued by critical race scholars for the two Indigenous stories that represent moments of violence and oppression. These act in counterpoint to the more positive affirmations in many of the non-Indigenous stories that show experiences that are more diverse and less stereotypical (Mathewson 2004). The two First Nations representations portray women as victims and men as oppressors. A challenge to this view of the work was made in 2004 when Aboriginal actor Leah Purcell produced a version of the *Monologues* with an all-Indigenous cast. It not only allowed her to redress the evenness of representation, but also to provide a space for the lesbian content in the play to be inhabited by Indigenous women, thereby creating diversity in representation, and turning an irrelevant and highly problematic text into a more palatable and relatable moment for the largely Indigenous community to which it was presented.

That there has been very little written about the lesbian experience in Aboriginal communities may reflect our numbers, but it may also represent the capacity for others to adequately represent diversity across our communities. A significant contribution to representing the moments of coming out is in Lou Bennett's one-woman performance *Show Us Your Tiddas!*, directed by Rachael Maza. The autobiographical production tells how Bennett witnessed violence in her community after someone's coming out and then decided to remove herself to a safer location to avoid the same happening to her. Bennett wonders if it is small-town Australia, rather than the specific Aboriginal experience, that resulted in the violence and exclusion. She ponders the fear, conveyed to some extent in Flanagan's article and also expressed in *Destiny in Alice*, that people will cast Aboriginality in a poor light because of a specific moment or event. This is challenged by the very act of Bennett presenting these concerns and a diverse experience, arguably something that would be difficult for someone outside of the culture to reflect.

This concern about expressing the complex lived experience of coming out, being out or speaking about being a lesbian, and how this can be manipulated by people like Flanagan to suggest a bias in the community, can present a risk for those of us who discuss the variety of responses. There are times when I am asked to speak freely to my own individual identity as an Aboriginal lesbian, but frequently the question when connected with Aboriginality is a more general question of how I am treated and if lesbian sexuality is an issue. I am immediately concerned that this question, as Willis (1992, p. 111) would frame it, is 'a declarative structure [that] has the function of a question'. Is it genuine inquiry or do they intend to affirm their own preconception that I am treated poorly? Like many Aboriginal lesbians, I cannot extricate myself from any of the markers that set me as an individual. Are there any ritual or cultural moments that I am excluded from as a lesbian? Apart from those same moments that my non-Indigenous counterparts face, such as a lack of access to marriage, accessible reproduction, adoption and some other basic human rights that the government denies all lesbians and gay men, I am largely no less excluded from ritual and celebration within my own Aboriginal community.

Are there specific issues that arise for Aboriginal gays and lesbians that do not exist for our straight counterparts? If a non-Indigenous partner has a child in the relationship, will the couple's child be able to secure Aboriginal identity? Our processes of Indigenous identification in Australia, it must be remembered, are also required and dictated by the non-Indigenous government (Carlson 2016), and the same processes of exclusion and difficulties of identity are shared by a range of peoples. The questions again become as complex as the individual, the community and the specific circumstances. If the question is more about how a community feels about me as a lesbian, this is a far more complex question around how any individual is treated within a community, and therefore a more difficult one to answer. In my own experience, when I have been shunned by members of my community – and it has occurred – it has been for the same reasons that Deborah Cheetham indicates, around a conflict between their religious beliefs and the challenge that my sexuality presents in that belief system. And, for me, this experience has been as common in the context of non-Indigenous peoples.

Ultimately, what do Aboriginal lesbians share that other Aboriginal women do not? If it were only the desire for the same sex, the whole notion that there needed to be a demonstrable moment of identity may seem irrelevant, but as a sexual identifier 'lesbian' has its own historical, political and cultural memory, which is managed by religion, the broader culture, the law and some of the significant markers mentioned earlier. We are not less Aboriginal for exploring and understanding this broad history. As Linda Tuhiwai Smith (1999, p. 33) argues, we must challenge the concept that accurate history has only one truth.

If Moreton-Robinson's *Talkin' Up to the White Woman* were mandatory reading for every well-intentioned neoliberal feminist, not least because it provides an eloquent preface for understanding how feminism itself is constructed, then *Colouring the Rainbow* and other texts that explore sexual diversity across First Nations Peoples should also be required to truly understand who we are as a people. In 2015 Aboriginal writer David Hardy gathered stories for an edited volume called *Bold: Stories from Older Lesbian, Gay, Bisexual, Transgender and Intersex People*. The book contained stories that detailed the lives of a range of 'mainstream' queer people and it included several stories from Aboriginal and Torres Strait Islander Peoples. This seamless inclusion may have occurred because of the Aboriginality of the lead author, but it is also becoming more common to expect our stories to be a part of the broader story of queer experience.

I share many moments with my straight Aboriginal sisters, but there are as many moments of divergence as there are convergence, and our communities are stronger for that diversity and richness of difference. This chapter has described some of the ways that we author and retell our stories as evidence that it is through this continued, persistent inclusion in the stories of the broader nation that we will gain traction. It is also a responsibility that we hold as women and as First Nations Peoples to actively listen to the lived experience of our diverse community and to demand that this diversity informs how the wider community engages and interacts with us.

BIBLIOGRAPHY

Baylis, T (2015) 'Introduction: Looking in to the mirror', in D Hodge (ed.), *Colouring the Rainbow: Blak Queer and Trans Perspectives – Life Stories and Essays by First Nations People of Australia*, Wakefield Press, Adelaide.

Bolling, R (2007) 'Hey, Kids! Interested in Science?', In *Tom the Dancing Bug*, viewed 12 April 2015, from <http://www.gocomics.com/tomthedancingbug/2007/12/29>.

Bonson, D (2016) 'Indigenous suicide, sexuality and gender diverse populations', *@IndigenousX*, viewed 1 May 2016, <http://indigenousx.com.au/indigenous-suicide-sexuality-and-gender-diverse-populations/#.Vz6NNbTmTqs>.

Cantor, C and Neulinger, K (2000) 'The epidemiology of suicide and attempted suicide among young Australians', *Australian and New Zealand Journal of Psychiatry*, vol. 34, no. 3, pp. 370–387.

Carlson, B (2016) *The Politics of Identity: Who Counts as Aboriginal Today?*, Aboriginal Studies Press, Canberra.

Cheetham, D (2001) 'Sunday Nights with John Cleary', ABC Online, 3 February 2001, viewed 1 February 2009, <http://www.abc.net.au/radio/programs/sundaynights/deborah-cheetham/7745818>.

Clark, M (2014) 'Against authenticity', *Overland*, no. 215, pp. 30–36.

Clark, M (2015) 'Are we queer? Reflections on 'Peopling the Empty Mirror' twenty years on', in D Hodge (ed.), *Colouring the Rainbow: Blak Queer and Trans Perspectives – Life Stories and Essays by First Nations People of Australia*, Wakefield Press, Adelaide.

Dare, S (dir.) (2007) *Destiny in Alice*, film, Australian Film Commission, Canberra, viewed 1 February 2013, <http://caama.com.au/catalogue/destiny-in-alice-2007>.

Dudgeon, P and Fielder, J (2006) 'Third spaces within tertiary places: indigenous Australian studies', *Journal of Community & Applied Social Psychology*, vol. 16, no. 5, pp. 396–409.

Dunn/Holland, W, Fletcher, M, Hodge, D, Lee, G, Milera, EJ, Saunders, R and Wafer, J (Gays and Lesbians Aboriginal Alliance) (1994) 'Peopling the empty mirror: the prospects for lesbian and gay Aboriginal history', in R Aldrich (ed.), *Gay Perspectives II: More Essays in Australian Gay Culture,* University of Sydney, Sydney, pp. 1–62.

Ensler, E (2001) *The Vagina Monologues,* Dramatists Play Service, New York.

Flanagan, M (2006) 'Is reconciliation dead? Or will white Australia finally listen?', *The Age*, 1 June, viewed 1 February 2013, <http://www.theage.com.au/news/in-depth/is-reconciliation-dead-or-will-white-australia-finally-listen/2006/06/01/1148956482247.html>.

Goudie, S (2015) 'Your story, our story: recollections of being Aboriginal and queer in the 1980s and '90s', in D Hodge (ed.), *Colouring the Rainbow: Blak Queer and Trans Perspectives – Life Stories and Essays by First Nations People of Australia*, Wakefield Press, Adelaide.

Hardy, D (2015) *Bold: Stories from Older Lesbian, Gay, Bisexual, Transgender and Intersex People*, Rag and Bone Man Press, Melbourne.

Hodge, D (ed.) (2015) *Colouring the Rainbow: Blak Queer and Trans Perspectives – Life Stories and Essays by First Nations People of Australia*, Wakefield Press, Adelaide.

hooks, b (1989) *Talking Back: Thinking Feminist, Thinking Black,* South End Press, Boston.

HREOC (Human Rights and Equal Opportunity Commission) (1997) *Bringing Them Home Report*, Commonwealth of Australia, Sydney. Mathewson, C (2004) 'Straight from the (private) part', *The Courier Mail*, (Brisbane).

Monaghan, O (2015) 'Duel imperatives: decolonising the queer and queering the decolonial', in D Hodge (ed.), *Colouring the Rainbow: Blak Queer and Trans Perspectives – Life Stories and Essays by First Nations People of Australia*, Wakefield Press, Adelaide.

Moreton-Robinson, A. (2000) *Talkin' Up to the White Woman: Indigenous Women and Feminism*, University of Queensland Press, Brisbane.

Roberts, J (2007) 'Songline of singing sister act', *The Age*, 15 May, viewed 2 February 2009, <http://www.theage.com.au/news/arts/songline-of-singing-sister-act/2007/05/14/1178995071373.html>.

Schiwy, F (2007) 'Decolonization and the question of subjectivity: gender, race, and binary thinking', *Cultural Studies*, vol. 21, nos 2–3, pp. 271–294.

Smith, L (1999) *Decolonizing Methodologies: Research and Indigenous Peoples*, University of Otago Press, Dunedin.

United Nations Permanent Forum on Indigenous Issues (2007) *Indigenous Peoples, Indigenous Voices*, viewed 2 January 2008, <http://www.un.org/esa/socdev/unpfii/>.

Willis, D (1992) 'Caught in the act: using the rank scale to address problems of delicacy', in M Coulthard (ed.), *Advances in Spoken Discourse Analysis*, Routledge, London and New York.

PROFESSOR DAWN BESSARAB is from the Bardi people on the Dampier Peninsula, the Kimberley, and the Yjindjabarndi people in the Pilbara, Western Australia. Dawn is a senior social worker and Indigenous health researcher with extensive experience in Aboriginal child protection, family and domestic violence, family support and community development and Aboriginal health research. Dawn graduated with her doctorate, entitled 'A Study into the Meanings of Gender by Aboriginal People living in both Urban (Perth) and Regional (Broome) Settings', in 2007 and since then has published extensively on her work.

INTERROGATING GENDER: WHAT'S RACE AND CLASS GOT TO DO WITH IT?

Dawn Bessarab

The feminist movement challenging patriarchy made great inroads into improving the status of women in Western society, yet as a movement it tended to see all women's experiences as universal. This position was very quickly challenged by black feminists (hooks 1989; Huggins 1991), who argued that the feminist movement failed to acknowledge the role of race and class in women's experiences. Until black feminists challenged this notion, there was little understanding that women of colour and women from different class backgrounds did not share the same worldview or experiences. In Australia Aboriginal women challenged the white feminist position on issues to do with sexual equality with their men (Behrendt 1993; Huggins 1991; Moreton-Robinson 2000). For Aboriginal women the issue was not so much about sexual equality as it was about racial and class equality in a Western, white-dominated society (Huggins 1991). Traditionally, feminist approaches to gender failed to address the role that racial and class differences played in creating unequal power structures for women. In Australia under colonial rule, Aboriginal women quickly became powerless and dislocated under patriarchy; women were subjugated, sexually exploited and treated as unequal.

This chapter will discuss gender through the experiences of Aboriginal women who consented to participate in a qualitative research project exploring their gendered experiences of growing up in their family and community. I attempt to unpack the relationship between gender, race and class by interrogating the multiple layers that connect women's experiences not only as gendered beings but also as racial beings.

To position this study within an Indigenous methodology that respects Aboriginal epistemologies and ontologies, it was essential to locate women's experiences within Aboriginal meaning systems that honoured the integrity of the stories being told. This research was a meaning-based study that attempted to understand the experiences of gender from the standpoint (Foley 2002; Moreton-Robinson 2013; Rigney 1997) of the Aboriginal women participants. An Aboriginal standpoint provides an alternative story of gender that recognises and acknowledges the intersections of race and class in the lives of Aboriginal participants. The diverse stories in this chapter represent women of different ages, language groups, classes and geographical locations. Seventeen of the 38 people who were interviewed in this study (completed in 2006) were women, with six living in urban (Perth) and 11 in regional (Broome) locations. Utilising the Aboriginal network, participants were recruited through a process of snowball and purposive sampling which considered the criteria of age, gender and socio-economic positioning. To protect the identity of the participants all names given are pseudonyms.

CULTURAL DISCOURSES

Because cultural discourses play a crucial role in influencing our beliefs and expectations of gendered identity, what people expect of their children will mean different things in different cultures. For young Aboriginal girls and boys these expectations cannot be considered outside of their cultural and social contexts. In Aboriginal society family is central to kinship relationships and very early in life a child quickly learns the importance of kinship and where they belong in the family system. Collard and colleagues (1994, p. 116) define kinship as 'a confederation of family groups or a large group of kin related people'. In Aboriginal society relationships are informed by social, spiritual and political avenues of communication, and are important because they form the nexus which connects Aboriginal families to each other, their community and the land. Through kinship relationships young children learn who they are, where they belong and what is expected of them as gendered beings.

Irruluma (2000, p. 177) suggests that the 'Aboriginal child ... grows in a cultural framework which has the elements of traditional and confining contemporary (Western) influences which interact on cognitive and intellectual development'. Today Aboriginal children learn about their masculinities and femininities within a multiracial, multicultural environment that combines Aboriginal and Western ways of knowing and doing.

Denborough (1996, p. 93) on gender said that 'our gendered identities are not formed simply through our families, nor simply through our peers, but through relations with individuals, communities, and institutions'. Buchbinder (1994, p. 2) talking from a Western position argues 'the masculine is what men in their immense variety do, just as the feminine is what women do, rather than what men and women are' . For the Aboriginal women in this study their femininities were not just about what they did but also what they were. Women talking about experiences of being female also talked about being Aboriginal; their stories of femininity combined with their stories of being Aboriginal highlighted how these experiences were inextricably interwoven. For Aboriginal women in this study, to talk about gender was to also talk about race. Race and gender when coupled with class, particularly the lower end of the economic scale, have a huge impact on how women experience their gender compared to other groups (Crenshaw, 1994). According to Moreton-Robinson (2000), women of colour are doubly marginalised under a hegemonic system that is dominated by whiteness.

STRONG ABORIGINAL WOMEN

Women talked about the many different influences that contributed to their identity. Some of the major influences were the roles of their mother, grandmothers and aunties, while other women also talked about how they learned things from their father, grandfathers and uncles. Participants highlighted that in developing their gender identity, women did not just learn from women; they also learned from men about being female. Learning about being female was a flexible process, transmitted through different relationships that at times involved female and male family members, Aboriginal and non-Aboriginal institutions and community.

The idea of strength in the development of Aboriginal femininity was a major theme emerging from the stories of women's experiences. Contrary to Western notions of femininity that have portrayed women as weak and dependent (Woods 2002), Aboriginal concepts of femininity in this study portrayed women as strong and independent.

The story from Martie (52 years) was about her mother challenging a devil wind that blew through their camp:

> *[My uncle] ... he said girl come here, sit down I want to tell you ... your mother ... she's a strong woman, he said, they was camping once and sitting down and this big wind [came], and everybody run from the wind, there was a fierce savage ... Janapee meaning devilish wind and he said your mother run and she got the shovel and run towards the wind, she's talking Nyungar ... and she threw the ashes at the wind and he said that wind turned and he said I saw that from my own eyes.*

Her mother's challenge drew admiration from the men in Martie's family and is now a family legend. Martie's story is a good example of how gendered identity can be influenced through stories that are passed down by family members. Martie learned from her uncle that not only was it acceptable for a woman to be strong but also a quality that was admirable, demonstrating the transferability of gender as a concept in that women not only learn from women but can also learn from men aspects of their femininity.

Theresa (48 years) also learned that women can be strong as well as feminine:

> *She (mother) never let us get out of hand to be a complete tom boy ... you can be strong but you can also be feminine ... she reminded us ... that girls didn't do certain things ... we didn't chop wood, we didn't whistle, we didn't go around fighting ... she taught us ... to cook, start taking care of a house.*

Theresa's mother encouraged her to be strong, a trait associated with masculinity, but she discouraged other masculine behaviours, such as chopping wood, whistling and fighting. While her mother taught her behaviours that were also associated with femininity in Western society, discouraging Theresa from fighting was an indication of the enculturation of colonisation on the changing roles and behaviours of Aboriginal women.

FIGHTING WOMEN

During this study I was travelling on the train when I overheard a fighting yarn between two Aboriginal teenage girls. The main storyteller was telling her friend about a fight she had had with another young girl who had 'rushed' her up (challenged) and 'called' her out for a fight. This young teenager said that the girl was 'jealousing' her for her man. What interested me in this gendered story was the girl's description of how her mother had not only taught her to fight, but in this instance had also joined in and helped her daughter to fight the other girl. Her friend nodded, confirming 'yeah she's always lookin' for a fight'.

This fighting story resonated with other fighting stories from some of the women participants in this study and from female and male friends in the community who had raised the subject of Aboriginal women and girls fighting. A male colleague in the entertainment industry described a fight that he had witnessed between a group of young girls against another girl. He said that the group had kicked, punched and pushed the girl to the ground, overpowering her and being quite vicious in their attack. What amazed my colleague was the mob mentality and the kind of behaviour he would have attributed to young males. Other community members since then have also raised concerns around girls fighting and the masculine characteristics of their fighting.

Listening to the fighting stories told by different women interrupted the dominant Western narrative that describes women as gentle and non-aggressive (Burbank 1994). Aboriginal women in this study talked about challenging and fighting as a behaviour that was not the sole domain of men. In Western society, non-Indigenous women fighting is usually associated with lower economic or working-class groups and not the middle to upper-class groups. Aboriginal women talked about teaching their children to stand up for themselves, which involved fighting when necessary, but could also mean challenging people if you were mistreated. Casi talked at great length about fighting and equated this with her stronger side, which she had learned from her mother:

> *You know mum's always taught us ... someone hits you, you hit them back no matter what even if you get flogged you know, still stick up for yourself ... I don't like fighting at all ... if I ever get into a situation I talk my way out of it or try to ... on the other hand if someone ever hits me I'd always hit back*

> *… fighting is something that you have to know, being Aboriginal because if you don't fight back they'll keep on picking on you, you know.*

Discussions with many Aboriginal peers both young and old have revealed the same belief; when someone calls you out for a fight, if you do not defend yourself they will keep 'picking on you' or making trouble until you do. Responding can take two different approaches: fighting back or ignoring and walking away. The problem in walking away is what concerned Casi; people will keep picking on you. The difficulty for Aboriginal people is how they manage the constant challenges for a fight if they choose to walk away.

Fighting among women is accepted in the Aboriginal community, particularly if someone is picking on you and you have to stand up for yourself. Standing up for yourself is often expected and failure to do so can be seen as weak. Standing up can involve fighting if you are hit or it can involve standing your ground and challenging whoever is threatening you as a person.

Mary (77 years) talked about getting in the boxing ring with her sister:

> *We had a boxing ring and a couple pair of boxing gloves … even S and I got in, I used to say to my sister, 'don't hit me hard' and she used to get stuck into me and I used to get stuck into her after that, one kick two punches.*

Mary's mother had told her that she used to fight with her sister (Mary's aunty) and that her mother (Mary's grandmother) used to let them sort it out between them. A girl fighting was not new in Mary's family and was something that happened all the time.

SOCIO-ECONOMIC DIFFERENCES

Another major issue affecting experiences of gender in the Aboriginal community was economic status impacting on the ability of Aboriginal families to maintain their quality of life. Around the time of the interviews, the Western Australian Council of Social Service said poverty was increasing and 'the proportion of the population living on less than 50% of the median income (OECD poverty line) had grown over the last ten years to 11%' (WACOSS 2008). For Aboriginal people '30% … are in income poverty and approximately 50% of Aboriginal adults rely on some form of welfare payment' (WACOSS 2008).

The influence of socio-economic positioning on gender identity is extremely problematic for Aboriginal families who live below the poverty line and whose only source of income is welfare. Aboriginal participants both young and old talked about how their level of income influenced what they could and could not do and what significance this had on their experience of gender.

Didley (65 years) talked about her changing socio-economic circumstances:

> *Today we are very much isolated in some senses, we don't see our children as much as we want to. We're scattered throughout, especially in the city; we're scattered and as you grow older you can't afford, you don't earn the same, you don't have the same living standards. Because of finance, there are definite changes in your life and one of them is getting out and seeing the children ... and money becomes a problem.*

Didley's declining economic status was beginning to affect her life and how she carried out her responsibilities as an elder in her family. As people get older they become increasingly vulnerable and dependent on their family (Boldy et al. 2002). The lack of adequate finances and declining status of elders in the Aboriginal community means that many of them are becoming marginalised not only in their own families, but also in the broader community. For elders like Didley, contact with family is extremely important to health and wellbeing as well as being essential in maintaining familial connections. Rapidly changing demographics in Aboriginal society means we now have a declining elder population and a growing younger population (Health Info Net 2015); looking after our elders to ensure their health and longevity is an urgent priority.

One of the major cultural differences between Aboriginal and non-Aboriginal, Western society is the valuing of elders. Non-Aboriginal society tends to value youth – as people get older they become less valued and redundant – whereas in Aboriginal society, as they get older Aboriginal women and men become valued for their wisdom and knowledge (see for example Metropolitan Local Aboriginal Land Council 2015). With the adoption and influence of Western lifestyles and values this is now changing. Elders are becoming less respected and there is a breakdown in cultural obligations of care and respect for older people. In some instances elders are being exploited by different family members for their income (Office of the Public Advocate 2005). Not having access to elders means that Aboriginal children are missing out on an important cultural pathway and elders are not being valued for the role that they play in furthering and maintaining cultural knowledge systems (Walker 1993). Aboriginal society is poorer with their absence.

Casi (20 years) talking about her family had a different story:

> *Another thing that's always made me strong too is because my mother was a sole parent ... we were never that well off, we were very poor ... we never got nice clothes, we never had top of the range food or you know we never went to a top of the range school or anything like that; but the thing is mum always made sure we had clothes on our back, food on the table and all the bills were paid.*

Despite being poor, this young woman's mother shaped her daughter's femininity by teaching her how to care and nurture her own family. The important things that Casi's mother taught her were not focused on money but were about relationships and responsibilities. Her mother taught her how to be strong and to prioritise the essential items needed to raise a family and survive.

Interrogating the intersection of class with gender, Casi's story reveals the issue of affordability for Aboriginal parents and the impact on young Aboriginal people in low-income families. Although Casi did not dwell on not having top-of-the-range clothes, the fact that she mentioned it indicates she was aware of it while she was growing up. If parents cannot afford the right clothes it often means that their children are marginalised within their peer group and in society. Not being able to fit in or meet the expectations of their peers or Western society can make Aboriginal children and parents extremely vulnerable within a Western system that places a high value on money and affordability, both of which can create barriers to accessing services and social inclusion. The impact of low socio-economic status on young people's self-esteem and confidence can be enormous, affecting their capacity to interact and engage as equals in both Aboriginal and Western society; 'Income is ... essential to meeting material as well as psychosocial needs, and poverty is a contributing factor to greater social exclusion' (Pyra Management Consulting Services 2006, p. 7).

Casi's story reveals the emerging class differences in Aboriginal society where some families struggle to meet their basic needs. This difference can and does affect how young people relate to each other and whether they can participate in mainstream activities that other groups take for granted. It also raises the question of what happens when parents are not able to meet their basic needs and put food on the table.

ABORIGINAL FEMININITY

Women in this study had similar views to Western society on the role of women as nurturers and caregivers. They talked about the importance of being there for their children, ensuring they were regularly fed, keeping a clean and tidy house and maintaining their child's health and hygiene. Some women added new responsibilities for Aboriginal women today, including teaching children how to stay safe and protect them from child abuse as well as making sure they go to school and receive an education.

Underpinning all this was the women's Aboriginal identity. Central to learning how to be women was learning about their Aboriginality. Women talked about learning to give and have respect for their elders, and about relationships and the importance of extended family in supporting and teaching them about their femininity. They learned from their grandparents, aunties and uncles concerning country, spirituality and the different responsibilities of caring for each other.

As Aboriginal women they described their myriad experiences of womanhood as a collage of extended family networks, cultural activities and spirituality against a background of racism, family violence, sexual abuse, alcohol and drug abuse and poverty. Their stories were balanced, reflecting the strengths of Aboriginal culture and what it meant to be woman as well as Aboriginal.

JEALOUSY

Another phenomenon emerging as significant in Aboriginal communities today is jealousy. Aboriginal people are talking about it more often and many attribute it as a causal factor in fighting.

During this study an article appeared in the *Koori Mail* (Shinn 2006, pp. 21–22) on the subject of jealousy. In the article Shinn talks about how she went out to a nightclub with her family and at this club, 'young Aboriginal women who she refers to as 'the sistas', jabbed, shoved and pushed her around all night'. When Shinn talked to her relatives about what had happened their response was, 'they were jealous ... that's just how it [is] with our mob, if you [dress] nicely and [are] confident, you [are] a target' (Shinn 2006, pp. 21–22). While pointing out that people can demonstrate their jealousy through verbal put-downs and accusing people of trying to be white, for example if you have a job or a house, Shinn also challenged the notion of jealousy. She was adamant that it was time for Aboriginal people to stop 'ripping into each other' and time to start supporting and being proud of being black.

Burbank (1994, p. 57) in her study with Aboriginal women in the Northern Territory said that 'the word 'jealous' was linked to aggression in women's conversation; at times it almost seems to be used as a synonym'. 'Jealousing' can occur over a range of different things:' men jealous women over men, women jealous men over other women, people can jealous other people for property, jobs, position/status, looks, education, privilege. Whatever the reasons, in this study Aboriginal women highlighted 'jealousing' as the main precursor to violence.

WOMEN AND ANGER

Burbank (1994) links acts of aggression to women's expression of being angry. In the Aboriginal community women and men have no difficulty in expressing anger, either at someone or something. Lerner, a psychologist writing about anger, says that it:

> *is a signal, and one worth listening to. Our anger may be a message that we are being hurt, that our rights are being violated, that our needs or wants are not being adequately met, or simply that something is not right.* (Lerner 1989, p. 1)

Martie's mother expressed her anger at the devil wind because she felt that something was not right. Anger can manifest as a verbal tirade or as a physical reaction and is not discouraged in Aboriginal society. In Western society women are taught to suppress their anger (Lerner 1989). Lerner (1989, p. 2) contends that Western women who show or direct their anger at men are condemned as "shrews,' 'witches,' 'bitches,' 'hags,' 'nags,' 'man-haters,' and 'castrators.' They are unloving and unlovable. They are devoid of femininity'. Similarly, Burbank (1994) expresses the view that anger is an emotion that is denied to women as 'emotional' beings, a view I find quite interesting, considering that in Western society, women are viewed as emotional beings, yet anger is the only emotion denied to them. Whereas men are encouraged to avoid being emotional because it is supposedly a feminine trait, anger is the only emotion that is seen as acceptable for men. The contradictions inherent in the rules around the manifestation of anger serve to highlight the complexity of different cultural rules.

During my 21 years of experience as an Aboriginal health and social work practitioner I have witnessed many angry Aboriginal women challenging the system or calling a fellow worker on an inappropriate comment. Often when Aboriginal women express their anger in white society it is mistaken for aggression and they then run the risk of being labelled 'out of control', 'aggressive' and 'anti-social'. Aboriginal women are regularly told that they should do an assertiveness course; assertiveness is seen as the panacea for anger and much more acceptable in dealing with conflict than expressing feelings of anger. Steps are taken to silence the voices of Aboriginal women who express their anger rather than listening to what they have to say.

RACISM

Another important factor that created problems for Aboriginal people in this study was racism. Women recounted both personal and generational stories of racism. Some generational stories had become folklore in their families. Thruppence (77 years) talked about growing up in Broome as a young person:

> *We weren't allowed to mix with, play with or have anything to do with the white kids ... when we used to go to the pictures we used to go way down the front and not go anywhere near where the white people was. The Asiatics was on one side, the white people in the centre and the half-caste on the other side and the native people way at the back.*

Broome in the early 1900s was founded on racial divisions and seating arrangements at the Sun Picture Gardens are well documented (Sickert 2003). Thruppence never questioned what was happening, she just accepted that was how things were. Her comment is indicative of how certain behaviours and actions become normalised around race.

Another participant, Lena (58 years), talked about her mother resisting police attempts to put her children on a truck and take them to the mission:

> *One of the stories that my sister told me, when my oldest brother he was a fighter, a registered fighter you know … and dad was away, this was the time they were taking us to the mission, and the policeman come there in his big truck and [said] 'come on get your kids on the back of the truck' … my mum was pregnant at the time … and he was abusive towards her … she didn't want to go … [the policeman] was pretty aggressive towards her … and because my mum didn't want to go … the policeman pulled his gun out and stuck it in her stomach and threatened to shoot her. My brother who was fifteen at that time, he … stood up to the policeman and told him to leave his mother alone and he was bashed with his gun and ah, knocked to the ground and knocked out … all the kids were chucked on the back of the truck.*

Lena's description is a powerful example of the intersection of race with gender and the impact of the dominant power structure on the lives of Aboriginal people in the early colonial days. Women and men were powerless and vulnerable under colonial policies. Lena's brother's attempt to protect his mother as the only male present resulted in him being struck down by a white police officer and bashed senseless. Lena's brother was seen as black first and deserving of the bashing for resisting authority, rather than as a young man protecting his pregnant mother.

The treatment of Lena's mother exemplified the complete lack of respect for Aboriginal women under a colonial regime and the lack of empathy for her pregnant status by the male officer when he threatened to shoot her and her unborn child. When we examine the experience of Lena's mother we see quite clearly how her race dictated her treatment. If Lena's mother and her children had been white, they would have been treated very differently.

More recently, speaking to a young Aboriginal girl on the train about her experience of racism, she replied,

> *all the time, me and my cousins walking down the street, cars go by and people call us boongs, dirty niggers and swear at us, my boy cousins, they rushed this one car up when they had to stop at the traffic lights; made them piss.*

Racism for Aboriginal people does not only occur in public places, it is also played out in institutions such as schools. Herbert (1995) found that many Indigenous girls suffered from low self-esteem as a result of the racist and sexist attitudes they were exposed to in the school environment. Girls revealed that being exposed to name-calling, including being called 'coon', 'abo', 'black bitch' and 'prostitute', did not make them feel good about themselves (Herbert 1995, p. 12).

Crenshaw, an African-American feminist, talking about identity politics, says that it becomes problematic when differences such as race and class are ignored in the experiences of women. She argues that, 'Although racism and sexism readily intersect in the lives of real people, they seldom do in feminist and antiracist practices' (Crenshaw 1994, p.32). When gender and race are viewed as separate and distinct from each other, Aboriginal people's identity as people of colour is a story that is silenced and constantly not heard.

DISCUSSION

Bloodworth (2000), discussing gender relations in early traditional Aboriginal society, argued that the context in which early explorers made sense of gender relations between Aboriginal women and men would have been based on the cultural beliefs and prejudices that they brought with them to the new land. Agreeing with Bloodworth, I don't believe very much has changed and that 230 years down the track, Aboriginal gender relations are still interpreted through Western cultural lenses and prejudices.

Despite colonial attempts to annihilate (Elder 2003), remove and assimilate people into white society (HREOC 1997), Aboriginal culture has survived and continues to thrive. The continuity of Aboriginal ways of knowing and doing were a recurrent theme emerging throughout the study. Aboriginal epistemologies of respect, spirituality, family, relationships and connectedness to land underpinned the gendered experiences of women in their families. These epistemologies continue to shape and influence Aboriginal concepts of gender that, coupled with Western expectations, influence how Aboriginal femininities are carried out and practised in multiracial, multicultural geographies.

Applying an intersectional approach to gender is to peel back the layers of Aboriginal gendered experiences to reveal not only the impact of race but also the additional burden of class and how this adds to the diversity of Aboriginal experiences. Today, while there are similarities in Aboriginal society to Western concepts of gendered behaviour, there are also differences; it is these differences that are often ignored in the application of policies, services and interventions in Aboriginal communities.

The different socio-economic positioning of Aboriginal people requires that if Aboriginal people from disadvantaged groups are to receive equal treatment and access to services, they may need to be treated differently and not be subjected to the one-size-fits-all approach. Megan Davis, Director of the Indigenous Law Centre at the University of New South Wales, commenting on welfare reform argued that,

> *When it comes to Indigenous issues, it is a one size fits all approach ... there is little cognisance of the remote and urban situations of Indigenous people ... Cape York communities are different to communities in Logan City, Redfern, Uluru or Perth.* (Davis 2005, p. 2)

Although we may share an understanding of what it means to be Aboriginal, we need to exercise caution in assuming that this understanding provides us with the right to speak for Aboriginal people from different socio-economic or geographical backgrounds. Today young Aboriginal people whose parents have successful careers or jobs are growing up in comfortable environments compared to a majority of their peers whose life choices are limited. These young people live in homes where there is high unemployment, criminality, poor education levels, alcohol, drugs and violence, hence their realities and stories will be very different.

Giving voice to Aboriginal women who represent these different layers within the Aboriginal community is essential if true representation is to occur. Although the commonality of Aboriginal identity suggests homogeneity, differences in language group and socio-economic positioning indicates that this is not the case. These differences highlight that the issues and social problems of women from different locations in Aboriginal society will be very different. Aboriginal women who have lower educational and income levels will have different issues to Aboriginal women who are well educated, employed and integrated into the mainstream community. Understanding how race and class can impact on Aboriginal people's experiences of gender is integral to working differently. Working with Aboriginal women needs to not only reflect culturally safe and secure processes of engagement but be appropriate and relevant in recognising the needs and differences of the group receiving the service. Recognising and acknowledging the role of race, class and gender in the lives of Aboriginal women can and does reveal a multi-layered story that is not homogenous and is complex in its diversity.

BIBLIOGRAPHY

Behrendt, L (1993) 'Aboriginal women and the white lies of the feminist movement: implications for Aboriginal women in rights discourse', *The Australian Feminist Law Journal*, vol. 1, pp. 27–44.

Bessarab, D (2006) 'A study into the meanings of gender by Aboriginal people living in urban (Perth) and regional (Broome) settings', unpublished thesis, Curtin University of Technology, Perth.

Bloodworth, S (2000) *Gender relations in Aboriginal society: what can we glean from early explorers' accounts?* viewed 7 November 2016, <http://www.anu.edu.au/polsci/marx/interventions/gender.htm>.

Boldy, D, Webb, M, Horner, B, Davey, M and Kingsley, B (2002) 'Elder abuse in Western Australia', report of a survey conducted for the Department for Community Development – Seniors' Interests, Curtin University, Division of Health Sciences, Perth.

Buchbinder, D (1994) *Masculinities and Identities*, Melbourne University Press, Melbourne.

Burbank, VK (1994) *Fighting Women, Anger and Aggression in Aboriginal Australia*, University of California Press, Berkeley and Los Angeles.

Collard, D, Crowe, S, Harries, M and Taylor, C (1994) 'The contribution of Aboriginal family values to Australian family life', in Inglis, J and Rogan, L (eds), *Flexible Families: New Directions in Australian Communities*, Pluto Press Australia, Leichardt, pp. 113–126.

Crenshaw, KW (1994) 'Mapping the margins: intersectionality, identity politics, and violence against women of color', in Fineman, MA and Mykitiuk, R (eds), *The Public Nature of Private Violence: The Discovery of Domestic Abuse*, Routledge, New York, pp. 93–118.

Davis, M (2005) 'Aboriginal leadership and welfare reform: you're not the first, Noel', *On Line Opinion,* 8 September, viewed 7 November 2011, <http://www.onlineopinion.com.au/view.asp?article =166&page=2>.

Denborough, D (1996) 'Step by step: developing respectful and effective ways of working with young men to reduce violence', in Mclean, C, Carey, M and White, C (eds), *Men's Ways of Being: New Directions in Theory and Psychology,* Westview Press, Boulder, pp. 91–115.

Elder, B (2003) *Blood on the Wattle: Massacres and Maltreatment of Aboriginal Australia since 1788* (3rd edn), New Holland Publishers, Sydney.

Foley, D (2002) 'An indigenous standpoint theory', *Journal of Australian Indigenous Issues,* vol. 5, no. 3, pp. 3–13.

Health Info Net (2015) *What details do we know about the Indigenous population?* viewed 7 November 2016, <http://www.healthinfonet.ecu.edu.au/health-facts/health-faqs/aboriginal-population>.

Herbert, J (1995) 'Gender issues for Aboriginal and Torres Strait Islander girls – exploring issues for Aboriginal and Torres Strait Island boys', *The Aboriginal Child at School*, vol. 23, no. 2, pp. 9–15.

hooks, b (1989) *Talking Back, Thinking Feminist – Thinking Black*, Sheba Feminist Publishers, London.

HREOC (Human Rights and Equal Opportunity Commission) (1997) *Bringing Them Home: A National Inquiry into the Separation of Aboriginal and Torres Strait Islander Children from Their Families*, Commonwealth of Australia, Sydney.

Huggins, J (1991) 'Black women and women's liberation', in Gunew, S (ed.), *A Reader in Feminist Knowledge*, Routledge, London.

Irruluma Guruluwina Enembaru (Isaac Brown) (2000) 'The socialisation of the Aboriginal child', in Dudgeon, P, Garvey, D and Pickett, H (eds), *Working with Indigenous Australians: a handbook for psychologists*, Gunada Press, Curtin Indigenous Research Centre, Perth.

Lerner, HG (1989) *The Dance of Anger: A Woman's Guide to Changing the Patterns of Intimate Relationships*, Harper & Row, New York.

Moreton-Robinson, A (2000) 'Troubling business: difference and whiteness within feminism', *Australian Feminist Studies*, vol. 15, no. 33, pp. 343–52.

Moreton-Robinson, A (2013) 'Towards an Australian Indigenous women's standpoint theory: a methodological tool', *Australian Feminist Studies*, vol. 28, no. 78, pp. 331–47.

Office of the Public Advocate (2005) *Mistreatment of Older People in Aboriginal Communities Project: An Investigation into Elder Abuse in Aboriginal Communities*, Office of the Public Advocate, Perth.

Pyra Management Consulting Services (2006) *Foundations for the Future: A Backgrounder on the Social Determinants of Health and Health Inequities*, The National Collaborating Centre for the Social Determinants of Health, Halifax, Canada.

Rigney, L-I (1997) 'Internationalisation of an indigenous anti-colonial cultural critique of research methodologies: a guide to indigenous research methodology and its principles', *Wicazo Sa Review*, vol. 14, no. 2, pp. 109–21.

Shinn, R (2006) 'Behaviour is not all right', *Koori Mail*, 18 January, pp. 21–22.

Sickert, S (2003) *Beyond the Lattice: Broome's Early Years*, Fremantle Arts Centre Press, Fremantle.

Metropolitan Local Aboriginal Land Council (2015) *Social and community role*, viewed 8 November 2016, <http://www.metrolalc.org.au/what-we-do/community/social-community/>.

WACOSS (2008) 'Anti-poverty week highlights hardship in WA', media release, Western Australian Council of Social Service, Perth.

Walker, Y (1993) 'Aboriginal family issues', *Family Matters*, no. 35, pp. 51–53.

Woods, JT (2002) *Gendered Lives, Communication, Gender, and Culture* (4th edn), Wadsworth/Thomson Learning, Belmont, California.

DR LYN HENDERSON-YATES is a senior Aboriginal woman from the Shadforth family in Derby in the Kimberley, Western Australia. She holds a Diploma of Teaching, Bachelor of Education, Master of Education and a Doctor of Philosophy and has worked in Aboriginal education for 38 years. In 2006, she took up an Associate Professorship at the University of Notre Dame Australia (Broome campus) as Associate Dean in the School of Arts and Sciences and establishing Director of the Nulungu Research Institute. In March 2009, she was made Professor and was appointed as the first Aboriginal Deputy Vice-Chancellor in Australia while remaining Director of the Nulungu Research Institute. In 2015, Lyn returned to Derby to take up the position of Chief Executive Officer with the Derby Aboriginal Health Service (an Aboriginal Community Controlled Organisation) and is also now an Adjunct Professor with the University of Notre Dame Australia.

'ARE YOU ONE OF THOSE THROW BACKS?' THE INVISIBILITY OF A FAIR-COMPLEXIONED ABORIGINAL WOMAN

Lyn Henderson-Yates

> *They cannot represent themselves; they must be represented.*
>
> Karl Marx (cited in Said 1995)

The question, 'Are you one of those throw backs?' was directed to me in early 2008. The speaker was a young Anglo-Celtic Australian woman speaking to me, an older Aboriginal Australian woman. To this young woman, I was invisible as an Aboriginal person. Langton (2005) asserts that, 'The easiest and most 'natural' form of racism in representation is the act of making the other invisible'. Questions such as that I was asked provide the context for this exploration into the questioning of Aboriginal identity by many people of Anglo-Celtic backgrounds. This chapter does not focus on the place of fair-complexioned Aboriginal people within Aboriginal society, nor does it examine the questioning of Aboriginal identity by people not of Anglo-Celtic backgrounds. The reason behind the decision to focus exclusively on Anglo-Celtic questioning is that I am using my own life experiences to explore whiteness and, at this point in my life, my experiences of identity questioning have come solely from people of Anglo-Celtic backgrounds.

This chapter explores my lived experiences as a fair-complexioned Aboriginal woman where I am frequently interrogated and silently analysed about my public identification as an Aboriginal woman. The first section of the chapter focuses on the concept of whiteness. The second section briefly describes my personal story, while the third section examines the motivation of those who make such assumptions and explores their underlying purposes. The conclusion highlights Aboriginal rights in self and community identification.

There have been many surprising and revealing questions, comments and statements expressed to me over my lifetime about my Aboriginal identity and I am still taken aback by each speaker's use of negative labelling, lack of propriety and cultural insensitivity. When Aboriginal people speak back to this questioning it is often seen as an overreaction and a strategy to create disharmony: a threat to the status quo.

COLONISATION AND WHITENESS

The concept of whiteness is essential when examining the role of identity questioning; it forms the basis of the white fellas who, consciously or subconsciously, use their position of white privilege to engage in identity questioning, thus continuing the colonising processes of domination and subjugation of Aboriginal Australian people. Stereotypical and limiting beliefs about racialised others have long been held in the Western world. Young quotes French philosopher Ernest Renan (1823–1892), who wrote about the characteristics and values of race and class, perceived as different and less than equal to his own European background.

> *The regeneration of the inferior or degenerate races by the superior races is part of the providential order of things for humanity. With us, the common man is nearly always a declasse nobleman, his heavy hand is better suited to handling the sword than the menial tool. Rather than work, he chooses to fight, that is, he returns to his first estate. Regere imperio populos, that is our vocation [and that] Nature has made a race of workers, like the Chinese race, who have wonderful manual dexterity and almost no sense of honour;*

> *govern them with justice, levying from them, in return for the blessing of such a government, an ample allowance for the conquering race, and they will be satisfied; a race of tillers of the soil, the Negro; treat him with kindness and humanity, and all will be as it should; a race of masters and soldiers, the European race.* (Renan, cited in Young 2002, p. 68)

Young (2002, p. 69) states that 'although he condemns conquests of one European race by another, Renan suggests that there is nothing shocking about the annexation of the country of an inferior race by a superior race – such as the British occupation of India'. Renan's beliefs are a prime example of the way in which the Western psyche convinced itself of its superiority over those it considered to be inferior.

Said talks about how being a white man (or woman) involved:

> *a reasoned position towards both the white and non-white worlds. It meant – in the colonies – speaking in a certain way, behaving according to a code of regulations, and even feeling certain things and not others. It meant specific judgements, evaluations, gestures. It was a form of authority before which non-whites, and even whites themselves, were expected to bend.* (Said 1995, p. 227)

Such beliefs have long held sway in many colonised countries, including Australia. Fortunately, in Australia, the number of Aboriginal people entering into discussions and debate about the colonisation of Aboriginal people continues to increase. Our ability to speak back is important, though we may be labelled or our words misused.

Dodson (1994, p. 10) writes that when we make known our self-representations to the public we can be exposed to 'appropriation and abuse' and that the way in which we express our cultural identities is often seen by the general public as an indication of our authenticity as Aboriginal people. Dodson states, 'However, without our own voices Aboriginality will continue to be a creation for and about us. This is all the more reason to insist that we have control over both the form and content of representations of our Aboriginalities' (Dodson 1994, p. 10).

Autobiographical narratives are one way we can make known our stories about our Aboriginal selves. Another method is to explore postcolonial theory, which provides a useful space for Aboriginal people to challenge the thinking and actions of an Australian nation that is slowly, and at times reluctantly, beginning to understand and perhaps deal with its past and present colonisation of Aboriginal people. It should be noted that many Aboriginal people were not compliant in the colonising process and resistance has taken many different forms over the years, from early armed resistance to writing exploratory papers. While, as Dudgeon (2007, p. 142) states, 'The term has come to mean many different things to many different people', postcolonial theory does provide an avenue to examine whiteness and find ways to speak back to the power of whiteness. The concept of whiteness, in this chapter, refers broadly to ethnocentric, taken for granted privilege that people enjoy socially and intellectually in a dominant white society (Moreton-Robinson 2004).

Many Australians would argue that Australia is no longer a colonising country and that Aboriginal people are no longer colonised. It is only when we remember that Australia is not a republic, that the Queen of Great Britain remains as its head of state, which is a historically symbolic social landmark, and that Aboriginal people continue to experience great disadvantage on every social, health and education level (HREOC 2008) do we realise that the ties and enactments of colonisation have not been broken. Colonisation continues to have a presence in Australia; often it is carried out through the ever pervading presence of whiteness.

If colonisation remains active, then it could be said that Australia is not entirely a postcolonial nation. Docker and Fischer propose that both Australia and New Zealand,

> *Are modern and post-modern at once. They are colonial (with regard to the treatment of their indigenous populations) and (as former British colonies) simultaneously post-colonial ... Their common political heritage – the distinctive constitutional mould of Westminster-style liberal, Parliamentary democracy – marks their traditional link to the Old World of European Enlightenment and to the West; yet, they are also distinctively part of the New World 'discovered', 'explored' and 'developed' by colonising Europeans.*
> (Docker and Fischer 2000, p. 5)

Unpacking the concept, expression and enactment of whiteness is crucial in exploring why many white fellas unquestioningly feel it is their right to challenge and question Aboriginal identity. Underlying whiteness are notions of privilege, power and quests for economic wealth. The Aboriginal voice challenging whiteness and its various forms of expression causes some discomfort to those who are actively engaged in perpetuating and maintaining power. Often many white fellas don't understand or accept what is meant when Indigenous people and people of colour talk about whiteness and its role in the oppression and continued suppression of non-white people.

Dyer wrote in *White*:

> *There are three senses of whiteness as colour, three ways in which it is felt and understood. First, white is a category of colour or hue, an observable distinction in the tints of the world, just like red or green. Second, white is a category of skin colour. Third, white, like any other hue, has symbolic connotations.* (Dyer 2007, p. 45)

Dyer's last definition of white represents most closely what is meant when I speak of whiteness. However, I suggest that white has not only symbolic connotations but, as a concept and a belief, also has a very real purpose and outcome. In so many ways, white is associated with ideas such as good, right, the pure, cleanliness, the brave, the civilised and so on. Connellan (2006, p. 1), in writing about the colour white in interior design, states that 'white as a colour is problematically conflated with light and its associated mythologies of goodness and cleanliness'. An integral component of whiteness is 'white privilege'. Hovane (2007, p. 8) in talking about 'colour blind services and practices' within work around family violence, stated that 'White privilege refers to the advantages and benefits that White people generally, including White feminists, derive socially and economically, as a result of being White'. McIntosh (1988) in her paper on white privilege talks about the many ways in which her whiteness provides her with advantages that are not as readily available to people of colour, such as being able to go into a shop knowing she will not be followed or the ability to rent or purchase a house in an area in which she chooses to live, knowing that she will be accepted because of her skin colour. McIntosh (1988) states she was 'taught to see racism only in individual acts of meanness, not in invisible systems conferring dominance on my group'. White, then, has definite purposes and a multitude of meanings, both symbolic and real.

GROWING UP AGAINST WHITENESS

While I have previously written of my childhood living in my hometown of Derby in the Kimberley (Rodriguez 2007), it is important to present a brief overview here so that whiteness is examined within real-life contexts. My childhood experiences revolved around my family; we were a large extended family who experienced the usual ups and downs of life as Aboriginal people living a low socio-economic lifestyle. My mother is Aboriginal and my father was a third-generation Australian of Irish and Scottish descent. I had seven other brothers and sisters; a younger brother has passed away and another younger brother has been listed as a missing person since 1974, aged 12 years, and, after an inquest, is now presumed to have been abducted and murdered. My stepfather was Yamaji from the Mid West region of Western Australia. I have two children; from their father's lineage their grandmother was Nyikina from country between Derby and Fitzroy Crossing, while their grandfather was Spanish. My three grandchildren have Anglo-Celtic fathers.

My grandfather, Harry Shadforth, was born in northern Queensland. At the age of six he and his siblings were sent to Mapoon Mission in Queensland. Government documents from 1904 record his removal to the mission as 'Harry, half-caste, six years, of Lawn Hills. Committed to Mapoon'. At 17 years, my grandfather was matched by the missionaries, according to skin colour, with my 16-year-old grandmother, who was also in the mission, and married; both were very reluctant as they were too young and did not like each other. During his years on the mission, my grandfather was trained to sail the mission lugger, taking supplies from the mission to Thursday Island. In 1920, in response to a request for a lugger and a skipper from Kunmunya Mission in northern Western Australia, my grandfather, grandmother and their two young sons sailed from Mapoon Mission to Kunmunya Mission. Over the next 20 years, my grandfather sailed the mission lugger to and from Broome carrying supplies and people. During this time, my mother and her further five siblings were born. My grandfather's family also extends across the top end of the Northern Territory and Queensland, from Borroloola to Cairns.

I was very fortunate to have grown up among my Aboriginal family and community in Derby. As a young woman, I didn't consciously think about the colour of my skin. I have a recollection of *knowing* I had fair skin but never saw myself as different to my mother, stepfather, brothers and sisters and close family and friends (Rodriguez 2007). Many times I looked at my skin and while I *knew* the colour was white, my inner self *saw* black and that black did not represent a colour but a culture, a people. It was a very comforting and secure feeling to be part of an all-embracing family and community. This sense of belonging remains a strong part of my being. However, it wasn't until I entered my mid-twenties and began to venture outside my community that I realised my Aboriginal identity was being challenged by white fellas.

It was at school that I had my first experience of an Anglo-Celtic person trying to work out where I fitted in the world of Aboriginal and white Australia. This attempt to define who I was took place in the local government school in Derby around 1969 when I was 12 years old. A public servant was attempting to work out the percentage of Aboriginal blood I had, but it wasn't until I was older and studying that I realised what he was trying to do. Talking with my mother a number of years ago, she said that in the late 1960s she had been told to go to the Native Welfare Office. The interviewing officer said to her that, happily, all her children could now be classified as white but she couldn't be because she 'fell below the mark' (Rodriguez 2007, p. 75).

I recall as a 14 year old, while attending high school in Perth, students laughed whenever I said I was Aboriginal. Often they wanted me to provide evidence of Aboriginality by asking, 'Say something in Aboriginal to me'. In 1982, I began studying an external bridging course to enter university. A publicity photo shoot of the Aboriginal students was organised in Perth to celebrate our completion of the course where we were grouped together facing the photographer. Of the entire group I was the fairest. Just before the photo was taken, I was asked by a staff member to step aside, away from the group. I was moved to the back of the room behind the photographer. Even after 34 years, I still recall the terrible feeling of exclusion. For some reason I blamed myself; I felt guilty but wasn't sure what I had done that was so wrong. It took all my effort not to cry in front of everyone. I was devastated and no one knew. I never saw myself as being any different to my Aboriginal friends in the group. It was only in later years did I understand that they wanted only students who obviously *looked* Aboriginal (Rodriguez 2007).

As an adult, white fellas respond to my identification as Aboriginal with gasps and comments such as 'But how can you be?', 'Why would you say you are Aboriginal?', 'Who are your parents? They must be very light' and

'Are you one of those throw backs?' For a long time, I just didn't understand why white fellas were continually challenging my identification as an Aboriginal person.

WHITE AUSTRALIA

The push for a white Australia began in the 1850s and progressed to the point where policies were developed to keep the country racially pure and free of undesirables; it wasn't until the early 1970s that such policies were finally discarded (Australian Government 2011). According to Prime Minister William Hughes (1919), the White Australia policy was 'the greatest thing we have achieved', while during World War II Prime Minister John Curtin stated, 'this country shall remain forever the home of the descendants of those people who came here in peace in order to establish in the South Seas an outpost of the British race' (Australian Government 2011). While the White Australia policy controlled who came to these shores, it also worked to control Aboriginal people and retain them in positions of servitude through protection and assimilation policies.

Gardiner and Bourke (2000, p. 47) propose that, 'The one constant in [the] process of representational schizophrenia, is the fixation of white culture with officially dominating and controlling Indigenous people, their identity and thus their futures – and with controlling the process of representation'. Attwood and colleagues (1997, p. 1) claim that, 'By the end of the nineteenth century, whites in the Australian colonies had a clear sense of themselves as superior to all non-European peoples, an idea buttressed by the apparent global dominance of European civilisation'. Haebich also highlights the longstanding place of whiteness in Australia:

> *Forged from successive waves of immigration into Indigenous lands, Australia is a society where whiteness – defined in terms of Anglo-Celtic culture and ancestry – has determined rights of citizenship, status, and belonging. We are the heirs of an unequal triangulated relationship where 'settler Australians' – defined here as the generations of migrants of Anglo-Celtic ancestry and their descendants from colonial times to the present – have been privileged over other immigrant groups and over Indigenous people.* (Haebich 2008, p. 10)

Such was the nation's commitment to designing and directing Aboriginal lives, that legislation was developed and implemented to ensure determinations of Aboriginal identity remained in the hands of the Anglo-Celtic majority. According to McCorquodale (1997, p. 4), since 1788 'no less than 67 identifiable classifications, descriptions or definitions have been used from the time of white settlement'. The classifying of Aboriginal people continues, with Groves stating that:

> *Even today indigenous peoples, on a daily basis, are subjected to non-indigenous scrutiny of their identity. Part of the problem is that many non-Aborigines continue to 'identify' Aborigines in terms of 'Wadjella-ness', that is, assessing Aboriginality by adopting non-Aboriginal criteria.* (Groves 2000, p. 139)

An Aboriginal person from a small north Western Australian town described a response from a new police officer who had just arrived in town from the city. The inference here is that the closer the skin colour of a person is to white, the closer they are to being a better citizen.

> *I look sort of white: when I told him I was Aboriginal he said, 'You must be one of the good ones then'. I thought about it and wondered, 'Is he being racist?' He just said it so matter of fact, like it was just okay to talk to me like that; he couldn't see anything wrong.* (Law Reform Commission of WA 2005, p. 32)

Dudgeon writes that,

> *The issue of Indigenous identity is the subject of ongoing and complex discussion by both non-Indigenous and Indigenous people [and that] Indigenous people are forced to continually define themselves within the backdrop of a dominant white historical, political and cultural context.* (2008, p. 173–74)

Indigenous engagement with challenging and speaking back to identity questioning is crucial in defending Aboriginal rights to cultural identity. Dodson argues that:

> *the insistence on speaking back and retaining control are highly political acts. They are assertions of our right to be different and to practise our difference. They refuse the reduction of Aboriginality to an object, they resist translation into the languages and categories of the dominant culture. They*

are at times ancient, at times subversive, at times oppositional, at times secret, at times essentialist, at times shifting. It is for this very reason that I cannot stand here, even as an Aboriginal person, and say what Aboriginality is. To do so would be a violation of the right to self-determination and the right of peoples to establish their own identity. (Dodson 1994, p. 10)

Facing up to identity questioners is often emotionally and spiritually exhausting but, nevertheless, speaking up must continue. Huggins summed up how many Aboriginal people feel about imposed identities when she stated:

I detest the imposition that anyone who is non-Aboriginal can define my Aboriginality for me and my race. Neither do I accept any definition of Aboriginality by non-Aboriginals, as it insults my intelligence, spirit and soul and negates my heritage. (Huggins 2003, p. 60)

NEGOTIATING IDENTITY

I also feel strongly about having imposed identities placed upon me. The issue for most non-Aboriginal people is that my fair-complexioned appearance and my identification as an Aboriginal woman does not match their ideas of Aboriginality; this is a challenge for they see before them a physical reflection of themselves. Roberts writes:

I hear some people ask, 'Why even worry about the Identity issue?'. I know of people who wouldn't even bother talking about such issues – they know within themselves who they are, and the people who are important to them and their existence also know who they are. But unfortunately ... others have historically decided to classify Indigenous people without our consent and by their categories – whether it be by colour, location, language, to what degree we practise traditional ways etc. (Roberts 1999, p. 49)

Most white fellas are looking for outward signs of Aboriginality. As Roberts states, this often equates to skin colour and the spoken language; the darker a person is the more Aboriginal they must be; the more Aboriginal language or the stronger Aboriginal accent when speaking English the speaker has, the more acceptable is that person's claim of Aboriginality. Fair-complexioned Aboriginal people identifying as Aboriginal throw many white fellas into confusion with the result that they often reject that person's Aboriginal identification or assume that it is a recent acquisition. They may view the

Aboriginal person with suspicion. Boladeras (2007, p. 61) wrote that, 'People who publicly espouse an Aboriginal identity might be accused of being too white to be Aboriginal, and thought to be doing it for some undeserved or unearned political or financial benefit'. Dodson describes succinctly this 'preoccupation with observing, analysing, studying, classifying and labelling Aborigines and Aboriginality' and the:

> *obsession with distinctions between the offensively named 'full bloods' and 'hybrids', or 'real' and 'inauthentic' Aborigines, continues to be imposed on us today. There would be few urban Aboriginal people who have not been labelled as culturally bereft, 'fake' or 'part-Aborigines', and then expected to authenticate their Aboriginality in terms of percentages of blood or clichéd 'traditional' experiences.* (Dodson 1994, p. 3)

The onus is always placed upon Aboriginal people to provide information, to prove, to give evidence about identity, cultural ways and history. White privilege enables white fellas to be positioned where they have the power and we have to facilitate their understanding. Aboriginal people are constantly asked to 'please explain'. It is not the responsibility of Aboriginal people to teach white fellas about unlearning beliefs about Aboriginal people and racism. In her book *Sister Girl*, Huggins (1998) wrote of an interview between herself and bell hooks where they discussed how many white women found it difficult to relinquish power and that those who acknowledged their racism had to go and find out themselves how to resolve it. That is, it is not up to Aboriginal women to find the solutions for people and provide, as hooks states in Huggins's (1998, p. 63) book, 'a shortcut' to unlearning racism.

One of the more recent challenges to my identification as an Aboriginal person was made through the seemingly simple comment, 'It must have been hard for you to live in an Aboriginal community'. This statement – she was not asking a question – was made by a white woman who had just met me. Although the person making the comment was female and was speaking with me, another female of a similar age, education and economic standing, the possibilities of a unifying sisterhood never manifested. This was a deeply embedded quest for greater power, dominance, privilege and superiority over me that was much stronger than her desire for unity as women. The speaker was not aware that this was the case, which makes it all the more worrying; that whiteness is so ingrained that careless comments can be made without consideration or reflection.

The speaker revealed the act of allocating her definition of Aboriginality to me and positioned herself as a 'gatekeeper' to both the Aboriginal and white worlds. This speaker sought to prevent me from entering the white-constructed, prescribed and protected zone that she considered to be the Aboriginal world. I was being 'bestowed' with the 'privilege' of being white without my desire or permission. I was being 'claimed' as white. I saw it as an attempt to dislocate my own sense of identity which sought to separate me from my family, my children and the Aboriginal community. It was also suggesting that I was not accepted by Aboriginal people; that I was without culture, connection and history. In this act, she tried to unmake me and in doing so shatter away from me the deep relationships that I am embedded in with my mother, brothers and sisters, my children, my uncles and aunts, my grandmother and grandfather and their families right back though time.

Conferring on me a white identity is no different to the government assimilation policies of the past. An attempt was being made to remove me from the Aboriginal world and place me into the white world without the need for legislation, resources or outcry. This cost-effective assimilation strategy may appear different from past legislation and practice but the desired outcome remains the same: the absorption of Aboriginal people into a white Australia.

Lake (2004, p. 44) showed that prominent Australian political leaders, at the turn of the 20th century, were 'determined to secure the white man's status and self-esteem in the south Pacific, by transforming Australia into a 'white man's country''. It is my view that, in their attempt to continue the process of whitening Australia, many white fellas, perhaps unconsciously, actively engage in deciding who is and isn't Aboriginal.

Moreton-Robinson (2004, p. vii) points out that, 'historically, Australian scholarship on 'race'' has not fully explored the 'privileged subject position, structural location or cultural practices of whiteness'. Engaging in acts of defining others is in itself a demonstration of racism. Holding views about others based on race distinctions can often result in acts of racism and racial discrimination. The International Covenant on Civil and Political Rights states that, 'all peoples have the right of self-determination. By virtue of that right they freely determine their political status and freely pursue their economic, social and cultural development' (United Nations 1966, Article 1). The Australian 1975 Racial Discrimination Act echoes this, as does Article 33 (1) of the United Nations Declaration on the Rights of Indigenous Peoples:

> *Indigenous peoples have the right to determine their own identity or membership in accordance with their customs and traditions. This does not impair the right of indigenous individuals to obtain citizenship of the States in which they live.* (United Nations 2007, p. 12)

The attempted unauthorised appropriation of my identity is an enactment of racial discrimination that tries to exclude and restrict my position within the Aboriginal community. This is clearly an abuse of my human rights, fundamental freedom and cultural rights to identity as an Aboriginal woman. Identity is all encompassing and includes profound understandings about who we are, which family we belong to, which country we come from, a shared history and future, shared cultural understandings and belongingness. Peters-Little (2000, p. 13) writes that, '[h]aving a sense of one's own Aboriginality depends very much upon the community with which they identify'. Aboriginal people are not all the same; attempts to make us one homogeneous group are unacceptable. We have many similarities but, equally, we are also different.

CONCLUSION

In spite of receiving many challenges to my identity as an Aboriginal woman, I remain firm in who I am. If there has been any identity struggle during my life, it has never been within myself or within my community; the struggle lies in those who question who I am. In looking back over the past 30 years, I can say with some degree of optimism that Australian society is developing a more mature appreciation and understanding of Aboriginal identity. Nonetheless, we must continue our dialogue about what it means to be who we are, Aboriginal and non-Aboriginal, and what it means to be a citizen of this country. My hope is that this nation will continue to grow in its ability to accept others without placing people under the racial microscope. It is often overlooked that whiteness carries the very real possibility of limiting the human potential of both the practitioner and the recipient of actions of whiteness. Identifying, examining and challenging whiteness and its partner, racism, explored in this chapter via my experiences of identity questioning, are powerful strategies in guarding against its ability to cause disruptions to Aboriginal people and to the development of this country called Australia – a nation which expounds the valuing of all peoples and cultures and claims to give all its citizens a 'fair go'.

BIBLIOGRAPHY

Attwood, B, Edwards, D, Markus, A and Schilling, K (1997) *The 1967 Referendum, Or When Aborigines Didn't Get the Vote*, Aboriginal Studies Press, Canberra.

Australian Government (2011) *Abolition of the 'White Australia' policy*, fact sheet, Department of Immigration and Border Protection, viewed 19 August 2016, <https://www.border.gov.au/about/corporate/information/fact-sheets/08abolition>.

Boladeras, J (2007) 'The desolate loneliness of racial passing', in M Perkins (ed.), *Visibly Different: Face, Place and Race in Australia*, Peter Lang, Bern, Switzerland.

Connellan, K (2006) 'White spaces', *ACRAWSA e-journal*, vol. 2, no. 1, viewed 19 August 2016, <http://www.acrawsa.org.au/files/ejournalfiles/87KathleenConnellan.pdf>.

Docker, J and Fischer, G (2000) *Race, Colour and Identity*, UNSW Press, Sydney.

Dodson, M (1994) 'The Wentworth Lecture. The end in the beginning: re(de)finding Aboriginality', *Australian Aboriginal Studies*, no. 1, pp. 2–13.

Dudgeon, P (2007) *Mothers of Sin: Aboriginal Women's Perceptions of Their Identity and Sexuality*, PhD thesis, Murdoch University.

Dyer, R (2007) *White*, 7th edn, Routledge, New York.

Gardiner, G and Bourke, E (2000) 'Indigenous populations, 'mixed' discourses and identities', *People and Place*, vol. 8, no. 2, pp. 43–52.

Groves, D (2000) 'To what extent is contemporary Aboriginal identity political?', in A Brewster, A O'Neill and R Van Den Berg (eds), *Those Who Remain Will Always Remember*, Fremantle Arts Centre Press, Fremantle.

Haebich, A (2008) *Spinning the Dream: Assimilation in Australia 1950–1970*, Fremantle Press, Fremantle.

Hovane, V (2007) 'White privilege and the fiction of colour blindness: implications for best practice standards for Aboriginal victims of family violence', *Australian Domestic & Family Violence Clearinghouse Newsletter*, 27.

HREOC (2008) *Close the Gap: National Indigenous Health Equality Targets*, viewed 1 January 2009, <https://www.humanrights.gov.au/publications/closing-gap-national-indigenous-health-equality-targets-2008>.

Huggins, J (2003) 'Always was, always will be', in M Grossman, (ed.), *Blacklines: Contemporary Critical Writing by Indigenous Australians*, Melbourne University Press, Melbourne, p, 60.

Langton, M (2005) 'Aboriginal art and film: the politics of representation', *Rouge*, viewed 15 October 2016 <http://www.rouge.com.au/6/aboriginal.html>.

Law Reform Commission of WA (2005) *Aboriginal Customary Law: Discussion Paper*, Law Reform Commission of WA, Perth.

Lake, M (2004) 'The white man under siege: new histories of race in the nineteenth century and the advent of white Australia', *History Workshop Journal*, vol. 58, no. 1, pp. 41–62.

McCorquodale, J (1997) 'Aboriginal identity: legislative, judicial and administrative definitions', *Australian Aboriginal Studies*, no. 2, pp. 24–35.

McIntosh, P (1988) 'White privilege: unpacking the invisible knapsack', in PS Rothenberg and KS Mayhew (eds), *Race, Class and Gender in the United States,* St Martin's, New York, pp. 165–169.

Moreton-Robinson, A (ed.) (2004) *Whitening Race*, Australian Institute of Aboriginal and Torres Strait Islander Studies, Canberra.

Peters-Little, F (2000) 'The community game: Aboriginal self definition at the local level', *AIATSIS Research Discussion Paper*, 10, viewed 19 August 2016, <http://aiatsis.gov.au/publications/products/community-game-aboriginal-self-definition-local-level>.

Roberts, J (1999) 'Introduction', in D Oxenham, J Cameron, K Collard, P Dudgeon, D Garvey, M Kickett, T Kickett, J Roberts and J Whiteway, *A Dialogue on Indigenous Identity: Warts 'n' All*, Gunada Press, Perth.

Rodriguez, L (2007) 'But who are you really?' In M Perkins (ed.), *Visibly Different: Face, Place and Race in Australia*, Peter Lang, Bern.

Said, E (1995) *Orientalism*, Penguin Books, London.

United Nations (2007) Declaration on the Rights of Indigenous Peoples, viewed 8 October 2008, <http://www.un.org/esa/socdev/unpfii/documents/DRIPS_en.pdf>.

Young, R (2002) *Colonial Desire: Hybridity in Theory, Culture and Race*, 4th edn, Routledge, London.

Legislation

Racial Discrimination Act 1975 (Cwlth), <http://scaleplus.law.gov.au/html/histact/13/6681/pdf/RDA1975.pdf>.

International instruments

International Covenant on Civil and Political Rights (1966), <http://www.unhchr.ch/html/menu3/b/a_ccpr.htm>.

DR VANESSA LEE is from the Yupungathi (Cape York Peninsula, Queensland) and Meriam (Torres Strait Islands) Nations, and has lived on the land of the Gadigal (Sydney, New South Wales) people for several years. She is a social epidemiologist, poet, public speaker, educator and public health, health sciences researcher in the Faculty of Health Sciences at the University of Sydney and a Director of the board of Suicide Prevention Australia. Apart from holding a number of expert advisory positions, Vanessa contributed to changing policies for the health and wellbeing of Aboriginal and Torres Strait Islander people as the first National Aboriginal and Torres Strait Islander Vice President of the Public Health Association of Australia (2012–2015). In 2016, Vanessa was invited to present her poetry at the Sydney Writers' Festival. Vanessa's creative and academic work is directed towards preventive health and linkages to services for Aboriginal and Torres Strait Islander people.

AS BLACK WOMEN DO: ABORIGINAL AND TORRES STRAIT ISLANDER WOMEN'S RESILIENCE

Vanessa Lee

The following poem, *As Black Women Do*, which I wrote in 2016, is a timeline reflection of the inequitable policies continuously placed on Aboriginal and Torres Strait Islander women. The cultural, spiritual connection that unites black women contributes to an undeniable resilience. It sets the context of this chapter and leaves us wondering how, after having been the subject of such inequitable disadvantage, are Aboriginal and Torres Strait Islander women able to stay resilient and still be the strong advocates for change that we are.

As Black Women Do

Birthing on country
family support
knowledge shared
traditions taught
suddenly denied
by those who colonised
and partook
in black vagina rapes.
Forced protection
from one's own traditions
raising of half-blood children
by women of the church
no Indigenous consultation
by policy omission.

Still, we rose …
as black women do

Spiritually united
not dying out
steered to assimilate
an act of a policy
that marginalised and excluded
ethnicity and race.
Strained international
political relations
to the rescue
noted a referendum well overdue
to be counted in the census
Indigenous identity
in numbers we trust
perpetuating inequality.

Still, we rose …
as black women do

Introduced to self-determination
a native title step
towards reconciliation
exposing the truth
of Aboriginal children
institutional abuse
shadows of genocide
incarcerating souls
an offering
of an apology truce.
Influenced
by a social justice report
identifying
a need to Close the Gap
is something for which we have fought.
An ambiguous strategy
Closing the Gap
pulled together
by those struggling
to walk the talk.

Still, we rose …
as black women do

Witnessing, blatant lying
Army answer to sacred children
Another, cultural undermining
Truth actually
'want the land for mining'
Repeat, mothers' children removed
Given, again to the
women of the colonised
forgetting those
already taken
now committing suicide.

In the mix
confused youth
interpreting incarceration
as type of initiation.

Still, we rise …
as black woman do

Fighting as
Grandmothers against removals
knowing our lifestyle choices
provides an opportunity
to close our communities.
Poisoned by water
from fracking –
greed, the major contributor
mother earth collapsing.
Watching our people dying
from diseases
defunding of services,
as it pleases.
Depression now takes hold
youth suicide
possibly highest in the world,
diagnosis mental instability
struggling to juggle
cultural realities
constantly betrayed
by gendered race relations
alcohol induced fortification.

Still, we rise …
as black women do

Culturally bonded
spiritually empowered

strength and resilience
valuable tools
with integrity
and generational humbleness
we are the drivers
backbone
visionaries
feelers
healers
leaders
prophetic
with degrees in silence-ness.

Our song lines
connect to the dreaming.
We live in community
Bush
Desert
Salt water
Fresh water
Rainforest
City
Wild country
Cold country
River country
Rock country
Hot country
guided by ancestors in unity
Up and
Up …
WE Will, continue to rise …
As Black Women Do

From creation our ancestors endured the changing environment of the earth, from extreme cold to extreme heat, adapting their lifestyles communally to survive. Coming from the oldest continuous living culture, knowing, from a scientific test, that my DNA goes back 45,000 years – and in some Aboriginal and Torres Strait Islander women it might go back even further – is a blessing as it is without doubt that our ancestral DNA prepared us unknowingly for what was to come with the onslaught of colonisation.

The policy decisions continuously made by national, state and territory governments, churches and other institutions, since colonisation, have contributed to unequal distribution of power and resources between Indigenous and non-Indigenous people and, inevitably, have had grim impacts on Aboriginal and Torres Strait Islander peoples' health and wellbeing (Fredericks et al. 2012; Kickbusch 2015; Mackenbach 2014). Consequently, Aboriginal and Torres Strait Islander women have lower socio-economic experiences than non-Indigenous women as a result of their life circumstances (Burns et al. 2013). This includes such things as 39% of Indigenous females being employed compared to 55% of non-Indigenous females, and less than 5% of Indigenous people obtaining a bachelor degree or higher compared to 20% of non-Indigenous people (Burns et al. 2013). The relationship between education levels and health outcomes is necessary to consider when addressing the social determinants as they are intrinsically linked to economic opportunity (Carson et al. 2007; Fredericks et al. 2012; Telfair and Shelton 2012). What this means is that the higher the achievement levels the more we see a reduction in societal disadvantage. Not addressing these social determinants in early life contributes to life-long disadvantage (Carson et al. 2007).

The social class structures that discriminate against Aboriginal and Torres Strait Islander women include race, sex/gender, ethnicity, Indigeneity and religion. These factors, amongst others, continue to place Aboriginal and Torres Strait Islander women close to the bottom of the ladder of socio-economic and political disadvantage. By understanding the interrelationships between the social structural causes of illness and health, governments would allow themselves the opportunity to recognise that the cycles of inequalities constantly placed on Aboriginal and Torres Strait Islander women makes it difficult to make positive lifestyle choices for future generations.

The constant failing of governments to take a holistic view, in addressing the social determinants of health, is evident in the life expectancy and health outcomes of Aboriginal and Torres Strait Islanders whereby 50% of the Indigenous population is under the age of 22 (AIHW 2015). Without a willingness to include Aboriginal and Torres Strait Islander women, towards understanding their cultural ways of doing, being and knowing, on policy decisions that affect their health and wellbeing and that of their children, there will continue to be no health equality for this population group.

The colonial humiliation, rapes, murders, identity theft, physical abuse, emotional abuse, genocide, and unhealthy responses to these, was and still is considered unnatural and not by any means has it been considered the 'norm' for our cultural way of life across any of our Nations. Having been raised by my Grandmother, I was always taught that for any inequitable predicament I encountered, our holistic lens would provide the necessary strategy that I needed to ride and stay above the waves. The holistic way to view the world enables the person to see the impact of their decisions and behaviour and that of others.

The knowledge that was once passed on by our ancestors only within Nations is now being taught and shared across Nations. There is a movement of genuine acceptance among Aboriginal and Torres Strait Islander women that our Nations have differing lenses by which to interpret or respond to a given situation – a necessary acceptance as colonisation has taken its toll. Each of our lenses is influenced by the environment and the interpretation of lore, from our ancestors and our families and communities today, in association with doing and knowing and being.

In the language of the Ngangikurungkurr people in the Northern Territory there is the Dadirri, inner deep listening and quiet still awareness, a way of life that encompasses the role of spirituality in Aboriginal culture (Ungunmerr-Baumann 2002; West et al. 2012). Dadirri is necessary for personal and social interactions as it is the interrelatedness between the past, present or future – situation or place – and spirituality or Indigenality (West et al. 2012). The following story is an example of how Torres Strait Islander women's lore was and still is taught. Fishing is a cyclic process that teaches deep listening and observing of the self and the environment and is a respectful awareness of the past, present or future that is learned over time. It is not about how big a fish is or how many fish you catch.

The afternoon before going fishing we would gather at my Grandmother's backyard. Standing closely around the fire my Grandmother would close her eyes and speak the old Meriam language softly to the dancing flames. As I felt the breeze circle us I could feel the sparks spring to life as my Grandmother's voice called on our ancestors to guide us to a spot of plentiful fish and a safe return. Upon recollecting ourselves she would tell us which side of the island was best to leave from, which landmark to align with when we got there, where the sun should be and which direction the current would be flowing as to where to throw our lines. She would also tell us the type of fish that we would be likely to catch. My Grandmother was rarely wrong. No-one spoke, we all just listened and when she had finished speaking we would nod in respect and prepare ourselves to go fishing in silence.

As day broke and the shades of pinks and oranges penetrated the sky we would make our way down to the boat ramp at back beach. There was rarely a word spoken and it was as though our energies were connecting with the crystal clear waters of the Torres Strait and the breeze, however slight. The boat would hum ever so softly across the still water like someone sliding across a glass ceiling careful not to disturb the fish.

When we arrived at the fishing spot we would all take turns to ensure that we were exactly aligned to drop anchor where my Grandmother had stated we should the afternoon before. Agreement was via a nod of the head and slight closing of the eyes. Then one of my aunts would lean over the side of the boat and place her palm flat on the surface of the water and say a quiet offering in language. The fishing would commence as each person was ready. Getting the timing right was evident in how much fish we did or did not catch. The air would then fill with the voice of one of my aunts who had something to share or something that was on her mind to discuss and about an hour later another aunt would respond and this one conversation on the same topic would continue for the whole length of the time spent fishing. Nobody spoke at once and if you couldn't contribute to the topic being discussed you just sat, listened and felt the rhythm of the waves as they lapped the side of the boat as though in union with the mood of the conversation.

We knew the fishing was finished by the reds, yellows and orange colours of the sun dancing their evening glows across the sky and the slight shift in the surface air of the sea. Upon leaving the fishing spot one of my aunts would lean over the side of the boat and lay her palm flat on the surface of the water and give thanks in language. Each person always gave a fish and any remaining bait back to the ocean. The responsibility of offering thanks was always to the eldest and should she be unable to do so the responsibility went down the line. The cleaning of the equipment and the fish was again done in silence. There was nothing to say. The fish was shared and hugs were given with the assurance that what was discussed during fishing remained with the fishing.

Fishing teaches you that the pace of life is better carried out in little dialogue, timing is everything, and we all belong communally. What happens to one of us affects all of us and, as Ungunmerr-Baumann (2002) states, 'there is nothing more urgent that we have to hurry for' and you cannot hurry or change the sea or the weather, you have to move with it, nor can you control the fish. It is about listening deeply to your surroundings to understand where you fit among all things and uniting spiritually as women in ceremony and celebration. This women's lore begins at a very young age and continues through the lifespan, preparing women with an understanding of how to cope with stressful situations in today's society.

The dominant culture in Australian society is the Western culture and this culture is represented throughout my poem, *As Black Women Do*, in the types of inequality placed upon Aboriginal and Torres Strait Islander people through policy aimed to control behaviour. The Western worldview has shaped Australian society and has attacked our cultural identity and knowledges as Aboriginal and Torres Strait Islanders (Rigney 1999), especially us as women. These inequitable attacks on us as black women, since colonisation, have resulted in our being labeled with the term 'vulnerability', a term used to reflect how we are not meant to be coping with the Western system and all the inequality of disempowerment and disadvantage thrown at us. However, the failure of Western society to understand how our ancestors genetically prepared us is its ignorance. The 'vulnerability' that Aboriginal and Torres Strait Islander women maintain is one of power. Aboriginal and Torres Strait Islander women's ways of doing, knowing and being should and can never be underestimated as we hold the survival and life promotion knowledges of our ancestors. The message in my poem of vulnerability as a power is very clear: 'still, we rise ... as black women do', 'WE Will, continue to rise ... as black women do'. Let's be the ancestors that our ancestors were to us.

BIBLIOGRAPHY

AIHW (2015) 'The health and welfare of Australia's Aboriginal and Torres Strait Islander peoples 2015', cat. no. IHW 147, AIHW, Canberra.

Burns, J, MacRae, A, Thomson, N, Anomie, Catto, M, Gray, C, Levitan, L, McLoughlin, N, Potter, C, Ride, K, Stumpers, S, Trzesinski, A and Urquhart, B (2013) *Summary of Indigenous women's health*, Australian Indigenous Health*Info*Net, viewed 27 December 2016, <http://www.healthinfonet.ecu.edu.au/population-groups/women/reviews/our-review>.

Carson, B, Dunbar, T, Chenhall, R and Bailie, R (eds) (2007) *Social Determinants of Indigenous Health*, Allen & Unwin, Sydney.

Fredericks, B, Lee, V, Adams, M and Mahoney, R (2012) 'Aboriginal and Torres Strait Islander health', in ML Fleming and E Parker (eds), *Introduction to Public Health*, 2nd edn, Elsevier, Sydney, pp. 350–72.

Kickbusch, I (2015) 'The political determinants of health – 10 years on', *BMJ*, vol. 2015, no. 350, h81, <http://dx.doi.org/10.1136/bmj.h81>.

Mackenbach, J (2014) 'Political determinants of health', *European Journal of Public Health*, vol. 24, no. 1, p. 2, <http://dx.doi.org/10.1093/eurpub/ckt183>.

Rigney, L-I (2001) 'Internationalization on an Indigenous anti-colonial cultural critique of research methodologies and its principles', *Wicazo Sa Review*, vol. 14, no. 12, pp. 109–121.

Telfair, J and Shelton,TL (2012) 'Educational attainment as a social determinant of health', *North Carolina Medical Journal*, vol. 73, no. 5, pp. 358–65.

Ungunmerr-Baumann, MR (2002) 'Against racism', *Compass*, vol. 37, no. 3, viewed 27 December 2016, <http://compassreview.org/spring03/1.html>.

West, R, Stewart, L, Foster, K and Usher, K (2012) 'Through a critical lens: indigenist research and the dadirri method', *Qualitative Health Research*, vol. 22, no. 11, <http://dx.doi.org/10.1177/1049732312457596>.